Signs and guiding for libraries

Signs and guiding for libraries

Linda Reynolds and Stephen Barrett

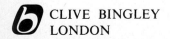
CLIVE BINGLEY
LONDON

First published 1981 by Clive Bingley Limited
16 Pembridge Road London W11
Set in 9 on 11 point Press Roman by Allset
Printed and bound in the UK by
Redwood Burn Limited of Trowbridge and Esher
Copyright © British Library 1981
ISBN: 0-85157-312-6

Text by Linda Reynolds and Stephen Barrett,
layout by Clive Bingley Limited, based on
original designs and illustrations by Stephen
Barrett

Contents

5

Acknowledgements

Research for this book originated at the Graphic Information Research Unit at the Royal College of Art, supported by a grant from the British Library Research and Development Department.

We should like to express our thanks to all the manufacturers and suppliers of materials, equipment and sign systems who sent us details of their products, and particularly those who were kind enough to lend us samples to photograph (see Chapter 3). Our special thanks are due to Letraset UK Limited, Mecanorma Limited and Colyer and Southey (Sales) Limited, who supplied us with substantial quantities of materials free of charge. These were used in the preparation of the two signing systems described in Chapter 4, and in the photographs illustrating Chapter 5.

We are very grateful to the Lyon Playfair Library at Imperial College for allowing us to use information on their signs as a basis for the two systems shown in Chapter 4. We should also like to thank the Science Museum Library and the Lyon Playfair Library for allowing us to photograph the signs on their premises. The staff in both libraries could not have been more patient or cooperative. During the course of this project we have also had informal discussions with a number of other librarians who have given us much useful information and advice. We are very grateful for their interest and their encouragement.

The photographs in Chapters 3 and 5 were taken by Paul Vonberg and Frank Thurston of the Department of Photography at the RCA, and we are greatly indebted to them for the care they took in producing results which would exactly meet our needs. We are also greatly indebted to Chris Perfect of the Department of Graphic Information at the RCA, who gave freely of his time to help with the legibility tests described in Chapter 4, and with sign manufacture.

Finally, we should like to thank Mrs Joan Eggleston, our Secretary, for the invaluable assistance she has given us in obtaining details and samples of products and for typing the manuscript.

Linda Reynolds and Stephen Barrett
London 1980

Introduction

The idea of producing this book arose from the results of a study carried out by the Graphic Information Research Unit for the British Library in 1977. The purpose of the study was to examine the state-of-the-art with respect to library graphics and to identify the major problems encountered by librarians in attempting to provide adequate library signing.

The study revealed that the general standard of graphics was poor. Rarely was there any attempt to coordinate the visual appearance of signs (including notices and labels), library publications and stationery, thereby creating a unified library image. In many libraries a variety of graphic styles had been used within each of these categories, and signs in particular tended to vary considerably in design and construction. Some libraries had clearly made an effort to improve the visual appearance of their signing, but had made fundamental design errors which could very easily have been avoided.

Two main reasons for this state of affairs emerged from the study. First, very few libraries had a member of staff with any design expertise whatsoever, and still fewer could afford to employ a design consultant. Graphics were therefore the responsibility of staff with little or no knowledge of basic design principles and techniques, or of the range of materials and production methods available to them. The result in many cases was inefficient use of the time of highly trained library staff and an amateurish end-product. Second, materials for the production of signs were considered to be expensive, and the cost of having signs manufactured outside the library or its parent organisation was often prohibitive. Sometimes, however, this was because the benefits of creating a visual identity for the library by means of a coordinated system of graphics had not been fully appreciated or accepted and the cost had not been budgeted for.

Large commercial organisations have long been aware of the advantage of creating a corporate image by means of a coordinated design policy for stationery, publications, signing, uniforms, vehicle liveries and so on. The same basic arguments hold true for libraries too. A strong visual identity will help both users and staff to regard the library as being well organised and efficiently run. Library signing is particularly important in this respect since it is a vital form of communication between the librarian and the library users. A logical and coherent system which is well designed, constructed and maintained is far more likely to generate confidence in the user than a haphazardly applied system with signs which are badly designed and manufactured and in poor condition. It will also save time for both staff and users and can only improve the relationship between them. Staff will find themselves spending less time answering trivial questions about the location of materials and services and how to use them, and they will therefore be able to spend more time giving specialist advice based on their professional training. By the same token, users with relatively simple requirements will be able to find what they need themselves without troubling staff, and those who do need professional assistance will find that staff have more time to give it.

While many librarians might acknowledge the strength of these arguments for a coordinated library image, the fact remains that the majority will still be unable to afford to employ a design consultant or to have large numbers of signs professionally manufactured. It seemed to us, therefore, that what was needed was a publication which would provide librarians with practical advice and information on the production of coordinated and pleasing systems of graphics at a reasonable cost. This book, we hope, fulfils that function.

Throughout the book we have stressed the importance of visual coordination. It is essential, however, that library graphics should also be coordinated in terms of their content. This is particularly important with respect to signs, which should be planned as a complete system. If they are put up at random as and when the need for them arises, there is a risk that information will be duplicated or omitted. In Chapter 1, therefore, we begin by considering the location and content of signs. We also suggest simple methods of assessing signing needs.

In Chapter 2 we go on to look at some of the basic principles of sign design. These are principles which will hold true regardless of whether the signs are produced professionally or in-house. They relate to the use of lettering, . arrows, symbols and colour, the layout of information on the sign panel and the placement of signs in the environment.

The various materials and methods available for in-house sign production are reviewed in Chapter 3. Off-the-shelf systems and production methods used by professional sign manufacturers are also discussed, and simple fixing methods are suggested for signs produced in-house.

In Chapter 4 we show how the basic design principles discussed in Chapter 2 can be applied in practice. Specific recommendations are made for lettering and panel layout, and these are illustrated by a series of photographs showing two signing systems in context. One of these systems would require professional manufacture, while the other demonstrates the use of materials and methods suitable for in-house production.

Some of the basic techniques which must be mastered in order to produce signs of a professional quality in-house are described in Chapter 5. We also give guidance on the preparation of specifications and artwork for the production of signs by a professional manufacturer.

Publications and stationery play an important part in creating a distinctive 'house style', and these are dealt with in Chapter 6. Production methods and basic design principles are discussed, and techniques in the preparation of artwork are outlined.

Finally, in Chapter 7, we look at some of the management aspects of a signing project. Much time and effort will be saved if the operation is planned efficiently. The importance of fully documenting the completed system in the form of a sign manual cannot be over-emphasised, and it may be desirable to undertake an evaluation exercise of some kind. Should the services of a professional designer be required, suggestions are made as to how a suitable person might be found.

These Chapters, then, should provide the librarian with much of the information he or she will need in order to create a system of library graphics of a professional standard. No book of this kind can hope to provide for every situation however, and some librarians will undoubtedly run across problems which require special treatment. What we have tried to do is to suggest general principles which will hold true for most situations, and we hope that the reasons underlying these principles will be sufficiently clear for the librarian to be able to adapt or extend them where necessary without jeopardising the system as a whole.

We should perhaps also emphasise that although we stress the value of creating a co-ordinated system of library graphics, we do realise that few well-established libraries will be in the fortunate position of being able to re-design and replace all signs, stationery and library publications at the same time. Nevertheless, we would argue very strongly that if, say, there is a need for new direction-finding signs or perhaps a new house style for library publications, then these should be designed in such a way that other kinds of library graphics can be coordinated with them in due course. It is almost always worth planning for a complete system, even if it can only be implemented in several stages over a number of years.

Chapter one Sign location and content

Before any serious thought can be given to the visual coordination of signs, the problem of coordinating them functionally in terms of their location and content must be considered.

Library signs fall into two major functional groups. There are signs associated with direction-finding, and signs relating to the use of library resources. The direction-finding system must set out to explain the overall size and shape of the library and the location of the various resources within it. It must then direct users to specific destinations by means of a logical progression of signs which give appropriate information where it is needed. Finally, the system must give users confirmation that they have reached their intended destination. Signs relating to the use of library resources must guide users in a logical fashion through the various procedures for using materials, equipment and services, and they must acquaint users with any special conditions or restrictions associated with the use of these resources.

There are certain general principles which can be applied in deciding where signs will be needed and what information they should give in order to function as a coherent system. It is important, however, that these principles should be backed up by a careful study of the way in which the particular library and its resources are —or will be—used. It will then be possible to draw up a complete list of the signs required, specifying their location and wording.

The signs must then be grouped according to their kind and their level of importance. In larger libraries, for example, it may be necessary to distinguish between primary destinations and secondary destinations within them. Until it is clear how many signs of each kind are needed and how much information they must carry, it will not be possible to make any decisions on their visual appearance.

Sign groups

Signs related to direction-finding

Plans These may be multi-level, showing all floors in the building, or they may show only one level. Multi-level plans present the user with an overview of the shape and size of the building, the spatial relationship between floors, and the location of primary destinations. Single-level plans are designed to help the user find his or her way around one particular floor.

13

The kind of labelling on the plan will depend on the amount of information to be included and the way in which the plan is intended to be used. For a relatively small number of destinations on each floor, it may be possible to label them by name on the plan. In most cases, however, a numbered key is likely to be necessary. The destinations on each floor should be numbered in some logical sequence, and the key can then either list these numbers in order, each followed by the appropriate destination, or it can list the destinations in alphabetical order and follow each with the appropriate number on the plan. The key is then functioning as a kind of directory.

Directories Directories are usually either floor-by-floor listings of primary destinations, or alphabetical listings. In the former case, as the name implies, the destinations will be grouped according to the floor on which they are situated. Each group will have a floor number associated with it. In an alphabetical directory, a floor number will be given with each individual destination name. In complex buildings it may also be necessary to specify which lift should be used. The alphabetical directory may be keyed to a floor plan, as suggested above.

Directories are also used for other purposes, for example to relate classmarks to stack numbers, or stack numbers to floors.

Directional signs These direct users to particular destinations by means of arrows. A directional sign may carry one destination or several. If there are several destinations, these will normally be grouped according to their direction.

Depending on the size of the library, it may be necessary to make a visual distinction between signs directing users to primary destinations (such as the reading room or stack area) and signs relating to secondary destinations within those areas.

Identification signs These serve to orient the user and to tell him when he has reached his destination. Under this heading we include external signs (such as those identifying the library, the main entrance and the car park), internal signs identifying primary and secondary destinations, and labelling on storage units and individual stock items. Several visually distinct levels of identification signs will therefore be needed.

Signs related to the use of library resources

Information signs These give the user information as to the availability of library resources, and any special conditions or restrictions relating to their use or to the use of the building in general. Information on opening hours, conditions relating to the borrowing of books and restrictions on smoking or eating in the library would be examples of signs in this category. Mandatory signs stating restrictions will often need to be visually distinguished from other kinds of information sign.

Information signs will usually consist of a short phrase or sentence, or sometimes a series of short sentences. Headings and subheadings may be required in some instances.

Instruction signs These are signs which guide the user through the procedures necessary for the efficient use of the library and its materials, equipment and services. Instructions as to what to do if there is a fire would also come under this heading.

Instructions usually take the form of a list of discrete statements, each corresponding to a stage in a procedure. Continuous text is rarely the best way of displaying such information. Diagrams are often included on instruction signs, particularly on those relating to the operation of equipment.

Sign location

Plans If the library consists of more than one building or is a very large building with several entrances, it may be necessary to display a plan at the entrance to the library grounds or in the forecourt. This will help users to find the appropriate building or entrance.

Inside the main entrance, it is helpful to display a simple plan of each floor. This will help users to see how the floors relate to one another and is particularly valuable in more complex buildings.

At other levels in the building, the relevant plan should be displayed near lifts, stairs and escalators. It may also be necessary to repeat the plan elsewhere on the floor in very large or complex buildings. An alternative to this is to have the floor plans printed in a leaflet which the user can carry with him, thus relieving the burden on his memory.

It is important that plans should be drawn and displayed in such a way that they are correctly oriented in relation to the building. Many people find it difficult to use plans, especially if they are required to mentally rotate them through 90 or 180 degrees.

Directories In a large library occupying several floors it will be necessary to display a directory of some kind just inside the main entrance.

Where the total number of destinations is relatively large, an alphabetical listing is often the best approach. Where the number of destinations is rather less, it may be more appropriate to list them floor-by-floor. Where there is a small number of destinations on only two or perhaps three floors, directional signs alone may be adequate. This will depend on the exact situation. In the larger library, however, the directory is the chief method of guiding the user to the correct floor for his destination.

The whole directory or the relevant part of it should be repeated on arrival at each floor, ie in lift halls and near escalators and stairs. Where a floor-by-floor listing is used at the entrance, this is best repeated in full on each floor. The information relevant to any particular floor can be graphically emphasised in some way, for example by the use of colour or image reversal. Repetition of the full directory on each floor in this way will help users wishing to go on to a second destination whose location they have forgotten or do not know. Where the total number of destinations is sufficient to merit an alphabetical directory, however, it is impractical to repeat the whole directory on each floor. A list of the relevant destinations only should then be given.

Directional signs Directional signs, together with plans and directories where necessary, should enable users to move from the main entrance to all primary destinations and then to secondary destinations within them. Users should also be directed back to the main entrance, to other exits and to vertical circulation points, and they should be able to move from one primary destination to another without difficulty.

In order to establish where directional signs will be needed, it will first be necessary to identify the primary destinations and the most direct routes to them and between them. Signing of alternative routes should be avoided as this may cause confusion and is likely to result in over-signing.

Signs should be placed at the 'decision points' on each route, ie wherever the user is faced with a choice of directions in which he might go. Signs which are not placed at decision points are likely to be ignored or the information forgotten by the time it is needed. As a general rule it should not be necessary to use confirmatory signs along a route which is properly signposted at decision points. Such signs will serve no useful purpose and will add to the apparent complexity of the system unnecessarily.

On large sites or campuses, external directional signs will be needed to guide users to the library. These signs will not necessarily be the responsibility of the librarian however. Directional signs pointing to the car park, main entrance, delivery bay etc may also be necessary if these are not immediately obvious.

Internally, directional signs may be needed to guide users from the main directory to the appropriate vertical circulation point. Once the user has reached the correct level, directional signs will then be needed at all decision points on that floor.

Identification signs Where the library occupies the whole building or has its own entrance, an external identification sign will be needed, simply to reassure users that they have indeed found the library.

Within the library, it will be necessary to identify each floor by means of a sign which is clearly visible as users arrive on that floor. It is particularly important that signs should be displayed opposite lifts, and they will also be needed at the top and bottom of all escalators and stairs.

All primary and secondary destinations referred to on directional signs will need to be identified, and in addition it will be necessary to label individual offices, toilets, areas to which the public are not admitted, and so on. Identification labels must also be displayed on storage units, and on individual stock items. In a library with a large stack area, it is especially important that individual stacks should be easily identifiable from a reasonable distance.

Information and instruction signs   Information signs must be displayed as close as possible to the point at which the information will be needed, or users will forget or ignore the message. It is important that information about hours of opening should be visible from outside the library as well as being displayed on the inside. Signs stating restrictions such as 'No smoking' or 'Quiet please' should be repeated as often as necessary in areas where the restrictions apply. Information relating to particular library resources should be displayed near those resources.

Instructions for using materials, services and equipment should be displayed as close as possible to the point of use.

Sign content

Information density

The golden rule with all signs is to give the minimum amount of information necessary to enable the user to find his destination quickly or to use a particular library resource efficiently. Superfluous information will compete for the user's attention and will merely serve to overwhelm, distract or confuse him so that he ignores, forgets or misunderstands the essential information. Where possible the wording should be brief enough for the sign to be read in passing. To stop and read a sign is a public confession of ignorance, and many people will keep moving regardless of whether they have had time to absorb the sign's message.

The amount of detail necessary on a plan will depend on where it is and how it is intended to be used. In general, however, there is little point in giving any more than primary destinations on multi-level floor plans displayed near the entrance. It may be worth increasing the amount of detail given on single-level plans however.

It is advisable to keep the total number of destinations listed on directories to a minimum. Too long a list is likely to discourage users and tempt them to ask for help rather than trying to find their own way. This will be particularly true for floor-by-floor directories where it will be necessary to scan through all of the destinations in sequence until the one required is found. In a large library, therefore, only primary destinations should be listed, plus any secondary destinations whose location the user could not be expected to infer correctly from the names of the primary destinations.

The information given on any directional sign should relate only to the action to be taken at the decision point where the sign is displayed. Information relating to subsequent decision points will tend to be forgotten and will merely serve to confuse the user. At some decision points—particularly those nearest the entrance or a vertical circulation point—the directional signs will need to carry several destinations. The number of destinations given at any one point should be kept to a minimum however. This is why it is important that the system should guide the user through the library in a progressive manner, directing him first to the primary destinations shown in the directory and only then to secondary institutions within them.

Identification signs present relatively little problem in terms of information density, since for the most part they will carry a single destination name.

With information and instruction signs, it is essential that the message should be concisely expressed, yet it should not be so brief that there is any risk of misunderstanding. Users are unlikely to bother to read lengthy information signs, particularly if they are merely stating

restrictions. Verbose instructions may be read, but often only when all else has failed. In the case of instructions, the length of the text can sometimes be reduced by the use of a diagram of some kind, for example to explain how to operate a piece of equipment. If the text cannot be reduced to a reasonable length, then it is questionable whether a sign is a suitable way of putting across the information. It may be that a printed leaflet or even an audio-visual presentation of some kind would be more effective.

Naming of destinations

It is helpful for the user if each destination name gives a clear indication of the materials or services available at that destination. When collections of books are named after the donor, for example, this gives the uninitiated user no clue as to the subject matter.

Destination names should be concise, but abbreviations of any kind should be avoided if possible. The use of initials for the names of departments is likely to be particularly confusing for the new user. If abbreviations cannot be avoided, they should be used consistently and not as a way of fitting a long message onto a panel which is too small for it. Providing that the system has been designed according to the principles suggested in this book, the librarian should never find himself in a position where he is tempted to do this. The panel size for signs of a given kind should be chosen to accommodate the longest message, rather than the message being cut to fit the panel.

In larger libraries it will often be helpful if a suitable generic name can be found for any destinations which have related functions and which are situated close together. The scope of any such names must be self-evident to users however. The generic terms can then be used for directional signing from the main entrance until the point at which the routes diverge. This will reduce the number of destination names needed on signs near the entrance, where the information load is always greatest. Where related destinations are not situated close together, as is often the case in older libraries which have expanded in a piecemeal fashion, it may sometimes be worth considering changing the location of one or more destinations. The more logical their arrangement, the easier it will be to guide people to them.

Once the destination names have been chosen, they should be used consistently throughout the entire signing system. If the same destination is referred to in different ways on different signs, then the user is likely to become very confused.

Numbering of floors

The numbering system used for floors or levels is likely to affect the ease with which the user is able to find a given level.

In buildings on sloping sites, a floor which is at ground level at one entrance may be the basement or the first floor at other entrances. The conventional system of naming floors as Basement, Ground, First, Second etc is therefore likely to be confusing. A more satisfactory solution is to designate one floor as the main horizontal circulation level. This would normally be the level on which the main entrance is situated. Other floors can then be numbered up or down in relation to this, which enables the user to orient himself more easily.

Wording of information and instruction signs

As a general rule, information and instruction signs should be worded as simply and concisely as possible. Words should be chosen carefully so that they convey exactly the meaning intended, and library jargon should be avoided. Once chosen, words should be used consistently so that the same situation, activity, procedure etc is always described in the same way.

Phrases and sentences should be constructed in such a way that no alternative interpretations are possible. This is sometimes difficult to achieve, but unintentional double meanings can provoke ridicule as well as confusion. In some situations it may be appropriate to omit certain parts of speech (such as definite articles) for the sake of brevity. This should not be done unnecessarily however, since the use of grammatically complete phrases and sentences usually results in a smoother flow of words. If too many words are omitted, the reader may find himself conscious of the clumsiness and ugliness of the sentence and, worse still, the message may become unclear. If it is decided to omit certain words, then this should be done consistently on all signs of a similar kind. As a general rule, sentences should be short, simple and direct.

It is also important to be consistent in the use of punctuation on signs. Unnecessary punctuation should be avoided, and full stops should not be used after headings or phrases which stand alone.

The emotional tone of the wording should be neutral as far as possible, and not threatening or provocative in any way. For permanent signs a reasonably formal approach is preferable, though a more informal tone may be suitable for certain temporary signs. Where possible, restrictions and instructions should be stated in a positive way rather than in a negative way.

The use of symbols

Symbols should only be used if they are likely to convey the intended message more effectively than words could do in a given situation, and/or if it is essential that the message should occupy as little space as possible. Their usefulness in a library environment is somewhat limited because so few of the activities which go on in a library are simple enough to be easily summed up by a symbol which will be unambiguous and immediately comprehensible to all. Even relatively commonly used symbols such as 'i' for information may not be recognised by all library users, and in some situations this particular symbol would not be precise enough. There is usually sufficient space available to display the word 'Information', and this will be more widely recognised and can be qualified as necessary. Some public libraries have experimented with the use of symbols to identify different subject areas, but it is difficult to arrive at unambiguous designs which will convey the same meaning to everyone. Even if the symbols are used in conjunction with appropriate descriptive terms in most situations, there will still be a risk of confusion where they are used alone, for example on the spines of books.

The most useful symbols are likely to be the man and woman conventionally used for toilets, and the symbol which indicates services or facilities for the handicapped. Although the man and woman symbols will often be reinforced by the appropriate words, used alone they can provide a convenient form of abbreviation where space is limited. This may be the case on plans, directories and directional signs.

Assessing signing needs

Information required

About users In order to determine exactly

where signs are needed and what they should say, it is necessary to know something about the users of the library, what they want from it, and where they are likely to encounter difficulties in using it. Questions to which answers will be needed include the following.

What are the characteristics of users in terms of age, occupation and cultural background?
This information is essential if an appropriate level of signing is to be achieved. The numbers of signs needed, the choice of words and the length and complexity of messages will all be affected. The particular requirements of staff should be taken into account in areas to which only they have access.

How frequently do users visit the library?
This will affect the level of signing needed. A library which is used mainly by regular visitors will not require such comprehensive signing as a library which has a continuous flow of new users.

Which are the most heavily used resources within the library?
On the basis of this information it will be possible to decide which resources (or destinations) should be given priority in the signing system. The terms used by visitors in describing their destinations should be noted, as these are the terms which will be most meaningful to them on a sign.

Do users encounter any difficulties in finding library resources or in using them, and if so, where and why?
These are perhaps the most important questions and the ones for which there are least likely to be answers already available. Knowledge of difficulties encountered by users will show where the present system of signing is failing, and may give some indication as to how it might be improved.

About the library It is also important to consider carefully certain characterisitcs of the library and its resources, since these too will affect the number of signs required and their content. The following characteristics are particularly important.

The nature of the building and the location of library resources within it
These will affect the direction-finding system in particular. In some cases it may be worth changing the location of certain resources in order to achieve a more logical arrangement, thus simplifying the task of providing adequate signing.

The number of different resources available and their physical size
Again, the direction-finding system will be affected by these factors.

The nature of the library's resources
The number and complexity of information and instruction signs needed will be affected by the nature of the resources. The use of a fiction

collection, for example, generally requires less explanation than the use of a collection of government reports or patents.

The procedures currently laid down or recommended for using particular resources
Careful examination of these procedures may suggest that they could be simplified in some instances. The more straightforward the procedures, the easier it will be to explain them to users.

Methods of obtaining information

The necessary observations of the library itself are, of course, relatively easily made, but to obtain adequate information about users, their requirements and their behaviour, it may be necessary to plan a small survey or experiment. Among the methods which might be used are the following.

Interviews Users might be interviewed on leaving the library, and possibly on entering it too. The questions asked of each user might include the following.
His (or her) age?
His occupation?
His first language if not English?
How often does he use the library?
Which library resources was he intending to use when he entered the library?
Did he have any difficulty in finding the resources he required, and if so where and why?
What routes did he take to reach those resources? Did he encounter any difficulties in using materials, services or equipment, and if so what were they?

The answers to these questions might be taken down more or less verbatim by the interviewer and the responses subsequently categorised, or the interviewer might be provided with a structured question sheet. For questions relating to topics such as the user's age and occupation, the frequency of his visits to the library and the resources he intends to use, it will be possible to specify the various categories of response on the question sheet so that the interviewer merely needs to tick the appropriate one. More complex questions are unlikely to lend themselves to this treatment however, and valuable information may be lost if an attempt is made to force users' answers into pre-defined categories.

Questionnaires Users might be asked to complete a questionnaire before leaving the library. This should be as brief and as simple as possible or they may be reluctant to fill it in. It should also be well designed and produced in order to give the survey an air of authority. Scarcely legible copies of a badly typewritten questionnaire are likely to be interpreted by users as being of very little significance. The questions themselves should be carefully worded so that users' responses are not biassed or unnecessarily restricted. As with interviews, it will be possible to categorise the possible responses to some of the questions and to ask users to tick the appropriate answers. With open-ended questions, it is important to give users a generous amount of space in which to write their answers.

Observation   The observation of users can provide valuable information about the shortcomings of an existing system of signing. In a large library it may be possible to follow visitors unobtrusively and then to interview them as they are leaving. Unobtrusive observation can be difficult however, and in many cases it will be necessary to invite users to cooperate. This may affect the behaviour of self-conscious users too greatly to yield any meaningful results, but some users may respond well to the situation and be willing to give a running commentary on their thoughts and actions as they move through the library.

Objective experimentation   In larger libraries it may be possible to run a small experiment to test the adequacy of an existing or proposed system of signing. Volunteers with little or no previous knowledge of the library might be asked to find specific resources in the library or to use certain materials, services or equipment. Their performance could be monitored by observing and timing them as they carry out the task and by questioning them afterwards.

Monitoring of enquiries   Staff might be asked

to monitor all enquiries and to take note of those which relate to direction-finding or to the use of library resources. This will help to establish where users are having difficulty and where they need more help from the signing system.

Specifying sign location and content

The first stage in deciding where direction-finding signs are needed is to list all the possible destinations which the user might wish to go to in the library, and to group them in a logical fashion into primary destinations subdivided into one or more levels of secondary destination. Areas or resources selected as primary destinations should include those most frequently referred to by users, even if they are relatively small in terms of the area they occupy. The position of these destinations should be marked on simple floor plans, together with the most direct routes to them and between them.

To some extent it will be possible to determine the decision points at which signs will be needed simply by looking at the plan, but each route should then be walked in both directions to make sure that no decision points have been missed. At each decision point it will be necessary to consider which destinations should be shown, and how many separate signs will be needed so that no matter what direction the user is approaching from, the information he needs is always immediately apparent to him. Information from users on any particular diffi-

23

culties encountered in direction-finding should be taken into account at this stage.

All points at which a sign is needed should be marked on the plans. It is helpful if different kinds and levels of sign are coded, for example A for plans, B for directories, C for directional signs etc. Each occurrence of a particular kind of sign can then be numbered (Cl, C2, C3, etc) and these numbers can then be keyed to a list giving the wording of each sign. A separate list should be made for each kind and level of sign.

The need for information and instruction signs should then be carefully considered, taking into account any particular difficulties encountered by users. The positions of these signs too should then be marked on the plans and keyed to a list giving the proposed wording.

The plan will now show at a glance the density of signs throughout the library and will indicate any points at which there are likely to be too many signs competing with one another. These areas can then be examined in more detail to see if the density of the signing can be reduced in any way.

The lists of wording for each group of signs should then be very carefully examined. The number of destinations shown on directional signs should be checked and an attempt made to reduce it if necessary. The wording of information and instruction signs should ideally be tested on a small number of users to ensure that the meaning is clear and unambiguous. Finally, the lists of wording should be carefully compared to ensure complete consistency throughout the system.

Chapter two **Principles of sign design**

In Chapter 1 it was suggested that library signs fall into two major functional groups; those associated with direction-finding and those associated with the use of the library and its resources. This grouping is also relevant to sign design, since direction-finding signs (with the exception of plans) consist of one or more destination names while information and instruction signs generally carry continuous or structured text. For convenience and flexibility, directories and directional signs are best made up of individual panels butted together, each panel carrying a single destination name on one or possibly two lines. Information and instruction signs, however, will generally be single panels carrying multi-line messages. These distinctions should be borne in mind, because although many of the basic principles of lettering apply equally to both kinds of sign, some of the broader aspects of sign design need to be considered specifically in relation to each of these two major sign groups.

Coordination and consistency

If library signs are to form a visually coordinated system, they must have certain design features in common.

All permanent signs, regardless of their kind, should be treated consistently in terms of their style of lettering and the basic principles used in determining the layout of the information on the panels. Colour should also be used consistently, and the number of different colour combinations kept to a minimum. Temporary signs may require slightly different treatment in

Cap height

Ascender

x height

Counter

Base line

Descender

Serif

some respects, but these too should be consistent among themselves.

Signs of the same kind and level of importance should have additional features in common. Wherever possible the size or sizes of lettering used, the size of the panels, the layout of the information on the panels and the position in which they are placed should be the same within any given sign group.

These common design features will ensure that all signs bear a strong visual relationship to one another, even though signs of different kinds may differ in their size and shape, in the size of their lettering, and possibly in their colour too.

Style of lettering

Choice of type face

Legibility Reading a sign at a distance of several feet is not the same thing as reading a printed page at a distance of fifteen inches or so. In choosing a type face it is therefore important to take into account certain aspects of type design which affect legibility at a distance.

As a general rule, the letter shapes should be simple and familiar for maximum ease of recognition. The x-height should be relatively large in relation to the capital letter height in order to ensure maximum legibility of the lower case letters, and the counters should be large and

open so that the internal shape of each letter can be readily distinguished at a distance. There should not be too great a variation in stroke width, or thin strokes may become indecipherable at a distance.

These requirements are perhaps best met by certain sans serif faces. Their simplicity of form promotes maximum legibility at a distance, and some designers feel that the letters are easier to space correctly than those of seriffed faces. Nevertheless, there are also seriffed faces which are perfectly adequate for signing.

Atmosphere value The choice of a seriffed or a sans serif face is likely to be determined largely by the nature of the building and by the kind of image which the library wishes to project.

Seriffed faces are felt by many people to be more suitable for older buildings, and they also tend to create a rather more traditional image. Sans serif faces, on the other hand, are particularly suitable for newer buildings with simple architectural lines, and they have connotations of modernity.

This is not to say, however, that a seriffed face will look out of place in a new building, particularly if it better reflects the desired image of the library. Similarly, a sans serif face may be appropriate in an older building if it says something about the character of the library.

The 'atmosphere value' of the type face can be modified to some extent by the colours used for the sign backgrounds and lettering. Seriffed

Grotesque

Optima

Helvetica

Folio

Standard

Futura

Gill Sans

A selection of sans serif faces which are suitable for signing.

A selection of suitable seriffed faces.

Plantin

Bookman

Melior

Clarendon

Jenson

Palatino

Alternative stencil faces.

ISO Stencil

OUTLINE

STENCIL

faces tend to look best with dark, subdued colours as these are most in keeping with the atmosphere created by the letter shapes, but sans serif faces are rather more versatile. For example, a sans serif face together with dark colouring might be suitable for a modern library housed in an older building or, conversely, for a more traditional library housed in a new building. A sans serif face together with a bright colour scheme would be ideal for a library in a new building wishing to create a friendly and dynamic image.

Coordination and availability In order to achieve the greatest possible degree of visual coordination between permanent signs, temporary signs, labelling and so on, the choice of type face must be considered in relation to the materials and methods to be used for sign manufacture. If all the signs are to be professionally manufactured the choice will be virtually unrestricted, but many of the materials suitable for in-house sign production are available in a limited range of type faces only. If some of the signs are to be professionally manufactured and some produced in-house, then the choice will be restricted to those type faces which are available for in-house sign production. However, if the materials and methods are carefully chosen, it will be possible to use the same type face throughout the system regardless of whether the signs are produced professionally or in-house.

If an attempt is being made to visually co-ordinate all library graphics, it is also important to consider the choice of type face for publications and stationery before making a final decision on the type face for the signing system. Few type faces which are suitable for use on signs will be unsuitable for printed matter from the point of view of legibility, though a lighter type weight may be required for publications. The question of availability will need to be investigated however. The choice may be limited either by the materials and methods to be used for sign production or by the typesetting system used for publications. If it is not possible to use the same type face for signs and publications, satisfactory results can be achieved by using type faces which are similar or by using the signing face for headings in publications and a contrasting face for the text (see Chapter 6).

Alternative treatments of the letter form

Most type faces are available in a number of different forms which may include italics, a range of type weights and a range of letter proportions. Not all of these variations are suitable for use on signs.

Italics Many type faces are available in an italic version as well as in the more familiar upright 'roman' form. Italics have been shown to be less legible than roman lettering for continuous text and the same is almost certainly true for signs too. This is partly because the italic letter shapes have less individuality and are therefore less easily distinguished from one another, and partly because we are less familiar with the appearance of italic lettering. The widespread use of italics on signs should therefore be avoided, though they may sometimes be useful as a means of distinguishing individual words or phrases on information or instruction signs.

Roman
Italic

Type weight   Type 'weight' is the term used to describe the thickness of the strokes making up the letter in relation to the size of the counters. Some type faces are available in three or more different weights, ranging from 'Light' through 'Medium' to 'Bold', 'Extra Bold' and even 'Ultra Bold'. These names are not used consistently however, and a weight which is called Medium in one face may be the equivalent of Bold in another. In selecting a type weight, therefore, it is important to look at examples rather than choosing on the basis of the name only.

For signing purposes a slightly bold weight is preferable, as this will be more legible from a

distance. If the type is too bold, however, the size of the counters will be reduced and legibility may be diminished. Medium or Bold will usually be the correct weight to choose, depending on the typeface.

On some signs it may be desirable to use a second, heavier weight of type as a means of emphasising headings or important words or phrases. If the Bold version of the selected type face has been chosen as the most suitable weight for the majority of the lettering, this may mean that there is no heavier weight available for emphasis. The alternatives in such a situation are either to use a different type face which has two suitable weights, or to use some other method of emphasising headings (for example, by using a larger type size or by means of space). Changes in type weight are the most satisfactory way of emphasising words or phrases within a piece of text, but capitals or italics may also be used.

Light
Medium
Bold

Letter proportion   Some type faces are available in 'Condensed' and 'Extended' (or 'Expanded') versions as well as in their 'Normal' form. These alternative versions are sometimes available in the same range of weights as the Normal version.

The Normal proportions are generally the most suitable for signing. With Condensed faces the letter shapes are not so readily distinguishable because of the reduced size of the counters, and from a distance adjacent letters may appear to run together. Extended faces have the disadvantage of having a longer alphabet length (ie they will occupy more horizontal space), which will mean that on many signs the message will run to an additional line.

Condensed
Normal
Extended

Capitals versus capitals and lower case

Research has shown that a mixture of capital and lower case letters is more legible than capitals only for both printed text and for signs. This is because the ascenders and descenders of the lower case letters result in more distinctive and easily recognised word shapes.

It is sometimes mistakenly argued that capitals will always be more legible from a distance because they are larger than lower case letters of the same type size. Lower case letters are certainly smaller, but this gives them the advantages of having a shorter alphabet length than capitals and of requiring less space between lines. This means that a larger size of lower case lettering can be used instead of capitals without occupying any additional space. The result will be considerably more legible than the same message in capitals only.

Capitals may sometimes be preferred for signs which need to convey an air of authority. However, if the text is more than two or three words (as in the case of instructions as to what to do if there is a fire, for example), then legibility will be reduced. In this situation it would be better to emphasise the importance of the sign by some other means such as colour. The use of capitals may also be acceptable in situations where a 'classical' atmosphere is required.

While lower case letters are recommended for the majority of wording, most users will prefer to see the use of capitals retained for the first letter of all proper names and for the first letter of the first word of any phrase or sentence. Not to use capitals in these circumstances will create an unfamiliar situation which may cause confusion. It is unnecessary, distracting and potentially confusing to use a capital letter for the beginning of every word however, unless each word is part of a proper name.

**TO FIND A BOOK OR PAMPHLET ON
YOUR REQUIRED SUBJECT LOOK
FIRST IN THE SUBJECT INDEX TO
FIND THE CLASSIFICATION NUMBER**

**To find a book or pamphlet on
your required subject look
first in the subject index to
find the classification number**

**To find a book or pamphlet on
your required subject look
first in the subject index to
find the classification number**

31

Long messages in capital lettering are difficult to read. If lower case lettering of the same type size is too small for good legibility at the required reading distance, then the best solution is to use a larger size of lower case lettering rather than capitals. The larger lower case letters need occupy no more space than the capitals, but they will be more legible as a result of their greater size and the more distinctive word shapes created by the ascenders and descenders.

Arrows and symbols

Arrows used on directional signs should be maximally legible from a distance, and they should also harmonise well with the type face. For good legibility, the free end of the arrow shaft should always extend well beyond the head. The head itself should be open rather than solid (because solid heads tend to be unnecessarily heavy in appearance, particularly when the arrow is pointing upwards), and the two lines comprising the head should always be at an angle of approximately 45 degrees to the shaft. If this angle is any smaller, the head will appear to fill in from a distance. The weight of the arrow should be adequate for easy recognition at a distance and should be appropriate for the weight of the type face. The construction of an arrow which will harmonise well with most type faces is described in Chapter 4.

Symbol shapes too should be chosen for maximum ease of recognition from a distance. As with lettering, the shapes should be simple and open or from a distance they will appear to fill in. The weight should be sufficient for good legibility, but not so great that symbols become the dominant feature of any sign panel on which they occur. The International Standards Organisation symbols satisfy most of these criteria. They are also relatively neutral in form and will therefore harmonise well with

most alphabets. The use of these symbols is described in Chapter 4.

Where arrows and symbols are used mainly for decorative purposes, as in graphic displays of various kinds, many of these constraints do not apply however. In this situation, immediate recognition from a distance is no longer a prime consideration and more elaborate or unusual designs are therefore permissible.

Size of lettering

Type sizes for printed information are usually expressed in points (1 point = 1/72in or 0.38mm). 'Point size' is in fact a measure of the body size of metal type, but it is also used in relation to photoset letters. In this case the point size is a measure of what the body size would be if the same type were cast in metal.

Different type faces of the same point size will not necessarily have letters of the same x-height, nor need they have the same alphabet length. Since it is the size of the letters themselves which is of the greatest significance for signing purposes, it is more meaningful to express type size in terms of the capital letter height in millimetres.

The minimum capital letter height necessary for good legibility in a particular situation will be influenced by the style of lettering used. Any

An arrow and symbols which are suitable for use on signs and which will harmonise well with both sans serif and seriffed type faces.

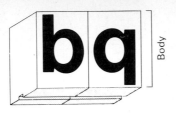

Body

deficiencies in the type face or letter form must be counter-balanced by the use of an adequate letter size. For any given type face and letter form, the size of lettering required for a group of similar signs will depend on the greatest distance from which signs in that group will need to be *read*; but remember that this distance will not necessarily be as great as the maximum distance from which they can be *seen*. Other factors such as the direction and level of contrast between the image and the background and the level of illumination in the library must also be taken into account. In addition, it is wise to make an allowance for users with less than perfect eyesight. There can be no simple formula for calculating the appropriate letter size for a given situation therefore. Simple tests on site, using lettering of the chosen type face, will be the most satisfactory way of determining what letter sizes should be used.

We have, however, attempted to provide some guidance on this question by carrying out distance legibility tests on a range of sizes for four different type faces. The results of these tests are reported in Chapter 4. It is likely that any type face similar to one of those tested (in terms of style and x-height to capital letter height ratio) would give comparable results, but nevertheless, great care should be taken in applying these data to other type faces.

Once the appropriate letter size for a particular group of signs has been decided upon, then that size should be used consistently for all signs in that group unless there is some very good reason for departing from it. Used in this way, letter signs can become a visual coding device which will help users to recognise particular kinds of sign. Differences in letter sizes must be substantial, however, or they will go unnoticed.

These words have been set in the type faces recommended on page 27. The capital letter height is the same in each case, but note how the x-height of the lettering and the length of the word vary from one type face to another.

Music Music
Music Music
Music Music
Music Music
Music Music
Music Music

Vertical alignment of lettering

The alignment of lettering against a left-hand margin requires care. If the first letters of each line are mechanically aligned by butting them exactly against the margin, letters with rounded shapes will appear to be too far to the right. Rounded letters should therefore be moved slightly to the left, so that the optical centres of the letters correspond. This is known as optical alignment.

Guides to published books

Mechanical and optical alignment.

Guides to published books

**dh
dr
no
oo
ov
rv
yv**

Letter spacing

The space between adjacent letters should be
just sufficient to clearly separate them. If the
spacing is too tight, the letters will appear to run
together when viewed from a distance. If the
spacing is too open, they will cease to hold
together as a word.

The spacing should also be consistent. It
should *never* be closed up or opened out merely
to make the length of the message fit the length
of the line. The need to close up letter spacing
in order to fit an over-long message onto a panel
of restricted size should never arise if the system
has been properly planned, and to open out
letter spacing to fill the available line length is
totally unnecessary and will produce a very ugly
result.

It is important that letters should appear to
be *evenly* spaced. This does not necessarily
mean that they will be *equally* spaced however.
Correct spacing is not merely a matter of leaving
the same distance between adjacent letters at
their closest points, because the letters differ so
much in shape. If all letters were equally spaced
in this way, then essentially circular letters such
as o, c and e would appear to be too widely
spaced and essentially vertical letters such as i,
l and t would appear to be too closely spaced.
It is the area of the space between letters rather
than the distance which is important. This is
best judged by eye, in which case the letters are
said to be optically spaced.

Some kinds of lettering designed for use on
signs require optical spacing but others have a
built-in system of 'mechanical' spacing. In
designing such systems, however, it is difficult
to take into account every possible combination
of letters, and with practice the spacing of
'difficult' combinations can be improved upon.
It is therefore important to learn to distinguish
between good and bad spacing. This is a matter
of developing a sensitive eye and of noticing
when the letters in a word appear to be evenly
spaced and when they appear to huddle together
in divisive groups.

It is worth noting here that capitals are much
more difficult to space satisfactorily than lower
case letters. This is yet another reason for avoid-
ing the use of all-capitals wherever possible.

Left: *These pairs of letters represent various
combinations of vertical, circular and diagonal
shapes, and each pair is correctly spaced. Note
how the spacing varies from one combination
to another, depending on the shapes of the
letters.*

36

Right: *Correct word spacing.*

Information
Information
Information

Tight, normal and open letter spacing.

ca**n**list
me kin
lse on

Word and line spacing

Word spacing should be sufficient to clearly separate words, but not so great that they cease to hold together as a line. With normal letter spacing, the correct word spacing will be approximately the width of the letter 'n'.

Line spacing must always be greater than word spacing, or vertical 'rivers' will be created and the text will become fragmented. The minimum acceptable line spacing is that required to prevent ascenders and descenders on adjacent lines from touching, but it is always best to err slightly on the generous side. If the spacing is too wide, however, the visual continuity of successive lines will be lost.

All-capital lettering will need slightly wider spacing than lower case lettering because of the greater x-height of the capitals. If lines of capitals are too closely spaced, their legibility will be much reduced.

Once chosen, it is important that both word and line spacing should be consistent rather than being varied according to the length of the message and the size of the panel. Any such variations will be immediately obvious even to the untrained eye, and they are likely to impair legibility as well as ruining the appearance of the sign. The importance of finalising wording and of preparing an accurate draft of the layout of each sign before commencing work on sign manufacture cannot be over emphasised (see Chapter 5).

To find a book or pamphlet on your required subject look first in the subject index to find the classification number

When line spacing is too tight in relation to word spacing, vertical 'rivers' are created.

To find a book or pamphlet on your required subject look first in the subject index to find the classification number

Here the relation between word and line spacing is correct, but both are too tight for good legibility at a distance.

To find a book or pamphlet on your required subject look first in the subject index to find the classification number

Here again the relation between word and line spacing is correct, but both are unnecessarily generous.

To find a book or pamphlet on your required subject look first in the subject index to find the classification number

Correct word and line spacing for good legibility on signs.

Justified versus unjustified setting

A piece of text is said to be 'justified' when both the left- and right-hand boundaries of the type area are perfectly straight. With unjustified setting, the right-hand boundary is ragged.

Justification of the right-hand margin can only be achieved by increasing or reducing the word spacing, and sometimes the letter spacing too, so that each line is exactly filled. From the foregoing comments on the importance of consistent letter and word spacing, it follows that justification of the right-hand margin is not recommended for signs.

Subtle variations in letter and word spacing may go unnoticed when justified setting is used in books, because the lines will be relatively long and the spacing will be increased or reduced equally along the length of each line. On signs, however, lines are generally much shorter and any differences in spacing will therefore be much more obvious. Furthermore, it is extremely difficult to achieve an even distribution of space along the length of each line by any method of lettering other than professional typesetting or the use of a sophisticated typewriter with a justification facility.

An additional argument against the use of justified setting on signs is that it may well result in an excessive number of broken words. Hyphenation too will be much more obvious on a sign than it is on a printed page, and should be avoided wherever possible.

Centred versus ranged-left layouts

Bearing in mind that unjustified setting is recommended for all text on signs, it is logical that headings too should be ranged left rather than being centred. With justified text it may be appropriate to attempt to centre any headings, but with text which has lines of variable length it is not. Centred headings may well be less legible too, since it is the natural tendency of the eye to return to the left-hand margin at the end of each line.

Ranged-left layouts are also more appropriate for direction-finding signs carrying lists of destinations. It is much easier for the eye to scan down such a list when each destination name begins at a predictable point on the line. With alphabetical lists, the search process will be considerably hindered if the first few letters of each name are not directly below one another for easy comparison.

There are also very good practical reasons for using ranged-left layouts. They are much quicker to produce than centred layouts, and much easier to produce well. The result is likely to be far more professional in appearance therefore.

Fire and accidents should be reported at once to staff at the information desk

Justified text.

Fire and accidents should be reported at once to staff at the information desk

Text ranged left, with the right-hand margin unjustified.

Fire and accidents should be reported at once to staff at the information desk

Centred text.

Line length

The optimum line length for signs in terms of the number of characters per line is considerably less than that for the printed page. This is because the lettering used on signs is generally much larger. The physical distance to be traversed by the eyes in reading a line of a given number of characters is therefore much greater, and there is a risk that the eyes will have difficulty in making an accurate back-sweep to the beginning of each successive line. Although the effect of the larger type size will be counteracted to some extent by the fact that signs are viewed from a greater distance than the printed page, this distance is not always great enough to compensate entirely. A shorter line length is therefore necessary.

For direction-finding signs carrying lists of destination names, twenty-five characters per line is a realistic maximum. Longer destination names will need to be split into two lines. For information and instruction signs, which generally carry text in a somewhat smaller type size than that used for direction-finding signs, a suitable maximum will be thirty to thirty-five characters.

Margins

Margins on signs should be relatively generous, to ensure that the information does not appear to be running off the edges of the panels.

On single-line panels used to build up directories and directional signs, the upper and lower margins should be equal and should allow ample space for the ascenders and descenders of the lettering. Upper and lower margins on identification signs can be more generous however, and in some cases wide margins will be desirable in order to create a panel of a substantial size. The left-hand margin should be of a standard width on all panels of the same kind, but the right-hand margin will vary depending on the length of the message in relation to the standard panel size for that group. The right-hand margin should be equal to the left-hand margin on the panel carrying the longest message. This will create a strong left-hand stress on all the other panels.

On multi-line panels (such as information and instruction signs), both the upper and lower margins should always be greater than the line spacing. The upper margin should be the same on all signs of the same kind, but the lower margin may vary where a common panel depth is used for several signs whose messages differ in length. The left-hand margin and the minimum width of the right-hand margin should be equal. Many lines will of course end slightly short of the right-hand margin, again giving a positive left-hand stress. Left- and right-hand margins should be standard for all signs of the same kind.

Where panels are designed to fit into frames or holders of some kind, an appropriate margin should be visible when the panel is in position. In the case of tier and shelf labelling, it may sometimes be necessary to use minimal margins in order to accommodate an adequate letter size, but the ascenders and descenders of the lettering should not touch the edges of the frame.

Panel sizes

Coordination

It is important that the total number of different panel sizes within the system should be limited. With single-line panels for direction-finding signs, all panels within the same sign group should be the same size. With information and instruction signs, all panels within the same group should have the same width and in some cases the same depth too. Panel sizes and proportions will differ considerably from one sign group to another, however, depending on the nature of the information. A common link will be provided by the principles used in

Administration offices →

Mens toilet ←

Heart pacemakers

There is a security system operating in this library

It is harmless to the general public but may affect a certain type of pacemaker

If you are wearing a pacemaker do not enter the library without contacting an official

Cases and bags

Cases and bags may be taken into the library provided that any books in them are shown on request

positioning the information on the panels (ie the internal dimensions).

The careful control of panel sizes will have a number of advantages. The use of a limited range of readily distinguishable sizes will produce a much more aesthetically pleasing result than the use of an arbitrary mixture of sizes. The effectiveness of the system will also be enhanced because panel size will become an additional cue enabling the user to distinguish between signs of different kinds at a glance. Furthermore, the use of a limited range of panel sizes will make for maximum convenience and economy in manufacture, no matter what method is used.

Calculation

The panel size required for a particular group of signs can be determined by adding together the amounts of space which will be occupied by the various visual elements making up those signs.

Although panel sizes will inevitably differ from one sign group to another, signs of the same kind and level of importance should have the same dimensions. With information signs, however, the panel depth may vary according to the length of the wording.

With directories, directional and identification signs, the standard panel depth will depend on the size of the lettering and the required depth of the upper and lower margins. The standard panel length for each group is best determined in relation to the length of the longest message in that group. Allowance must also be made for a standard left-hand margin, for a standard amount of space between wording and any arrows or symbols, and for a minimum right-hand margin. The right-hand margin on the panel carrying the longest message should be equal to the left-hand margin.

With information and instruction signs, the panel width for each group will depend on the size of the lettering, the chosen line length and the width of the margins. The panel depth will depend on the space occupied by each line of lettering, the number of lines of lettering, the space occupied by headings and the depth of the upper and lower margins. The depth will therefore vary according to the length of the wording, but the common width will provide a sufficient degree of visual coordination. Where two signs from the same group are to be placed side by side, however, they should both have panels of a depth determined by the length of the longer message.

One of the simplest ways of dealing with panel sizes is to base all panel dimensions on some multiple of the x-height of the lettering. This system is very helpful in determining appropriate panel dimensions for closely related groups of signs which differ in the size of their lettering. Single-line panels for directories and directional signs are examples of such groups. If the panel depth and the width of the side margins are calculated in terms of the x-height of the lettering and the same specification is used for both kinds of panel, then a strong visual relationship will be created even though the panels will differ in size.

The calculation of panel sizes is described in more detail in Chapter 4.

Panel layout

Plans

The simplest kind of floor plan is an orthographic or two-dimensional representation, drawn to scale. The positions of the structural features and major items of furniture are shown in outline only.

The oblique projection is a slightly more complex kind of plan which attempts to represent the features of each floor in three dimensions. It is a very simple extension of the orthographic plan, as the accompanying illustrations show.

Depending on the angle of projection used, the viewer's apparent vantage point will either be above and to the left or above and to the right. The best angle to use will therefore depend on the location of any important but minor features which might be obscured by certain angles of projection. Forty-five degree projections should be avoided however. We rarely see objects from exactly this angle, and as a result the plan will be unrealistic in appearance and will not give a strong three-dimensional impression.

The depth of walls etc must be sufficient to create a three-dimensional effect, but not so great that the floor is no longer visible in small rooms and narrow corridors. It is impossible to avoid partially obscuring features which are on or against the far side of any walls which are horizontally oriented on the plan. If these features are important, the wall can be broken to show them.

The three-dimensional effect created by the oblique projection is greatly enhanced when shading is used to give vertical surfaces solidity. Where it is desirable to show more than one floor on the same plan, the use of two oblique projections at an angle will help to crate an impression of superimposition.

Bearing in mind the need for the correct orientation of plans, the orthographic representation has the advantage of flexibility in the sense that it can be turned through 90 or 180 degrees without any loss of meaning or risk of confusion. This means that copies of the same basic unlabelled drawing can be used wherever a plan is needed. Each copy must then be labelled appropriately for its orientation, but if a numbered key is used, the same key will serve for all situations and only the numbers will need to be added to each copy of the plan individually. Direct labelling is in any case inadvisable, as there is rarely sufficient space.

The oblique projection has the advantage of giving a three-dimensional impression which some users may find easier to understand than the simple orthographic plan, but it has the disadvantage that it cannot be freely rotated. Depending on the projection used, it will be possible to rotate a horizontally drawn plan through 90 degrees in one direction only. If the plan is rotated in the opposite direction, it will appear to be upside down. It will therefore be necessary to re-draw the plan for certain locations. As with the orthographic plan, the use of a separate numbered key will reduce the amount of labour involved in producing the drawings.

Directories

As suggested in Chapter 1, there are two basic information layouts for major directories: either the destinations may be listed floor-by-floor or, if the total number of destinations is too large for this treatment, they may be listed alphabetically.

Floor-by-floor directories The floor-by-floor directory comprises a series of lists of destinations, each list being associated with a floor

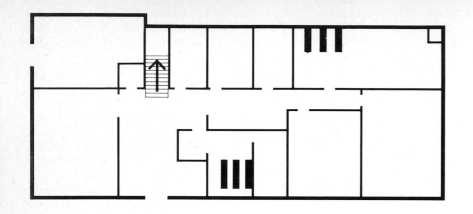

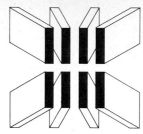

Above: *The oblique projection is very flexible and can be drawn at any angle and to any depth.*

Top left: *An orthographic plan.*

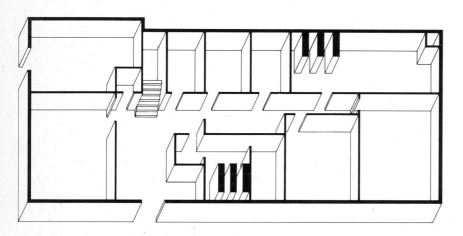

Bottom left: *An oblique projection, drawn from the orthographic plan.*

44

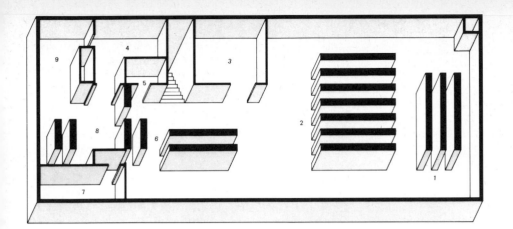

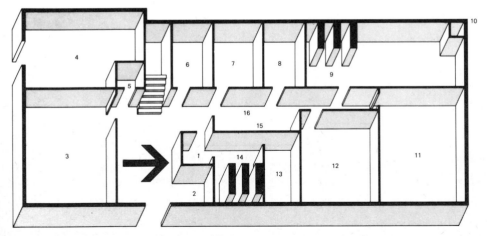

Oblique projections can be used to show the spatial relationship between features on different floors. Note how the use of shading reinforces the three-dimensional impression.

45

Anthropology	3
Astronomy	3
Bibliography	2

Computing science	3
Economics	3
Education	4

2	Biochemistry
3	Biology
3	Chemistry

Three alternative positions for floor numbers on alphabetical directories.

Alternative layouts for alphabetical subject directories. In a classified directory the classmarks would, of course, be given on the left.

Accountancy	657
Aerodynamics	533.6
Applied Mechanics	629.7

number. These lists may be placed one below the other, with the list for the highest floor at the top, or they may be placed side by side with the lowest floor on the left. The vertical arrangement is more usual and perhaps more easily understood, but the horizontal arrangement can be useful in situations where there is insufficient space for a vertical format.

The floor numbers can either be placed above or beside each list. They will need to be emphasised by their size, colour or position so that they stand out clearly from the destination names, and it should be immediately obvious which list each number refers to. Over-emphasis of the floor numbers can often provide an attractive graphic feature.

The destinations for each floor can be listed alphabetically or in some other logical order, but where there are only three or four on each floor it is often appropriate to arrange them on the basis of line length in order to create a pleasing appearance. Where possible it is best to alternate long and short lines, rather than allowing all of the short destination names to fall at the top of the list and all the long ones at the bottom or vice versa. All destination names should, of course, be ranged left.

If the whole directory is to be repeated on

Biochemistry	531.6
Biology	577
Botany	57

621.5	Control engineering
621.5	Electrical engineering
621	Mechanical engineering

each floor, the information relevant to the floor on which the directory is situated should be emphasised in some way. This could be achieved by reversing the direction of contrast on the panel carrying the floor number, or indeed on all of the panels relating to that particular floor. Alternatively, a different colour might be used for the panel backgrounds or lettering (depending on whether light lettering is being used against a dark background or vice versa). In some situations it may be desirable to include arrows on the panels relating to the floor on which the directory is situated. In this case the order in which the destinations are listed will normally be dictated by the direction in which they lie (see p50), and the same order of listing should be used on every directory. It must also be remembered that the use of arrows will increase the standard panel length for the directory.

If the relevant part of the directory only is to be displayed on each floor, then no colour coding will be necessary. The layout of each sub-directory should exactly mimic that of the main directory. Again, if arrows are included on the sub-directories, this will determine the order in which the destinations are listed and it will also affect the panel length.

Alphabetical directories If an alphabetical sequence is used, the main directory at the entrance will consist of a continuous series of destination-name panels, possibly with a deeper panel at the top carrying a heading. The destination-name panels should be designed on exactly the same principles as panels for a floor-by-floor directory, except that space must be allowed for floor numbers.

The floor numbers can be ranged left, ranged right or placed immediately after the destination name. A layout in which the numbers are positioned on the left is in many ways the most aesthetically pleasing, and the floor number for any given destination can almost certainly be located more quickly than if it were positioned on the extreme right of the panel. Placing the numbers immediately after the destination names is a compromise. Whichever arrangement is chosen, the position of the numbers in relation to the wording and/or the margins must be consistent.

The sub-directories on other floors will consist of an initial panel confirming the floor number, followed by an alphabetical list of destinations to be found on that floor. The design of the sub-directories should be similar to that of the main directory, though it may be appropriate to use a slightly larger size of lettering and hence a larger panel size. In some situations it may be desirable to include arrows on the sub-directories. In this case, the destinations should be grouped according to their direction.

Minor directories With directories linking information such as subject headings and class-

5	Librarian
	Library administrative offices
	Cataloguing department
	Aquisitions department
4	Tensor Society
	Operational Research Society Library
	Life science collection
	Mens toilet
3	Periodicals and abstracts
	Computing and control collection
	Womens toilet
2	**Main book collection**
	Restricted loan collection
	Mens toilet (facilities for the disabled)
1	Information
	Issue and return counters
	Catalogues
	Reference books and bibliographies
	Micro-readers
	Photocopying services
	Womens toilet (facilities for the disabled)

5	Librarian
	Library administrative offices
	Cataloguing department
	Aquisitions department
4	Tensor Society
	Operational Research Society Library
	Life science collection
	Mens toilet
3	Periodicals and abstracts
	Computing and control collection
	Womens toilet
2	Main book collection
	Restricted loan collection
	Mens toilet (facilities for the disabled)
1	Information
	Issue and return counters
	Catalogues
	Reference books and bibliographies
	Micro-readers
	Photocopying services
	Womens toilet (facilities for the disabled)

Two kinds of floor-by-floor directory.

The complete directory may be given at each level, with the relevant information emphasised in some way (left). Here the emphasis is given by image reversal.

Alternatively, the complete directory may be given at the entrance level (centre), with only the appropriate section repeated on other floors (right). Note that the size of the floor number has been increased on the sub-directory. This will ensure immediate recognition when the signs are placed opposite lifts.

2	Main book collection
	Restricted loan collection
	Mens toilet (facilities for the disabled)

marks, classmarks and locations (or shelfmarks) etc, the most common design fault is the use of unnecessarily wide spacing between columns of information. The spacing should be just sufficient to clearly separate the columns, but not so great that there is a risk of users making mistakes in reading across between them. Column spacing should never be opened out so that the information fills a panel of a given width. If it is desirable that the panel should be relatively wide in order to conform with other signs of a similar kind, the columns are best ranged left under a heading which is also ranged left, rather than being centred.

Sometimes, however, wide column spacing

First directory:

5
Librarian
Library administrative offices
Cataloguing department
Aquisitions department

4
Tensor Society
Operational Research Society Library
Life science collection
Mens toilet

3
Periodicals and abstracts
Computing and control collection
Womens toilet

2
Main book collection
Restricted loan collection
Mens toilet (facilities for the disabled)

1
Information
Issue and return counters
Catalogues
Reference books and bibliographies
Micro-readers
Photocopying services
Womens toilet (facilities for the disabled)

Second directory:

5
Librarian
Library administrative offices
Cataloguing department
Aquisitions department

4
Tensor Society
Operational Research Society Library
Life science collection
Mens toilet

3
Periodicals and abstracts
Computing and control collection
Womens toilet

2
Main book collection
Restricted loan collection
Mens toilet (facilities for the disabled)

1
Information
Issue and return counters
Catalogues
Reference books and bibliographies
Micro-readers
Photocopying services
Womens toilet (facilities for the disabled)

Third directory:

2
Main book collection
Restricted loan collection
Mens toilet (facilities for the disabled)

results from extreme variations in the length of items in the first column. In this case, column spacing can often be reduced by reversing the position of the columns. Thus an alphabetical list of subject headings, each followed by a classmark, will be easier to use if the classmarks are given first.

Directional signs

If there are directional signs which carry more

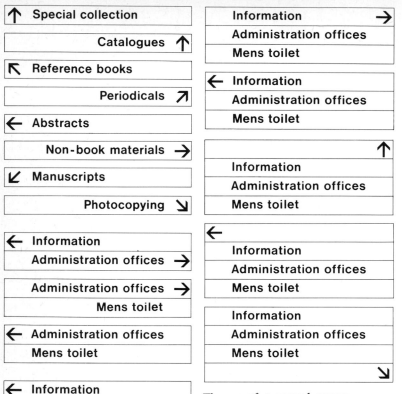

The use of staggered arrows.

With single directional panels, the destination name may be ranged left or right according to the direction in which the arrow is pointing. Note the order in which these single panels are arranged—this is the order in which arrows

than one destination name, as there will be in the vast majority of systems, the destinations should be grouped according to their direction. It will then be necessary to decide on an order of priority for arrows pointing in different directions. A suitable order would be to place destinations with upward pointing arrows first, followed by those with diagonal upward arrows, horizontal arrows and diagonal downward arrows. (The downward pointing arrow is unlikely to be needed, since it is conventional to use an upward arrow for 'straight on'.)

The arrows on directional signs may all be placed to the left or to the right of the destination names, or they may be staggered according to the direction in which they are pointing. There is probably little to choose between these

should always occur where several panels are butted together.

Where there are two destination names, these should be ranged left if they lie in different directions. If they both lie in the same direction, however, the two names may be ranged either left or right as appropriate, and it will not be necessary to repeat the arrow on the second panel.

Where there are three or more destinations the names should always be ranged left. If all the destinations lie in the same direction, the arrow need not be repeated. A separate panel can then be used for the arrow if desired.

50

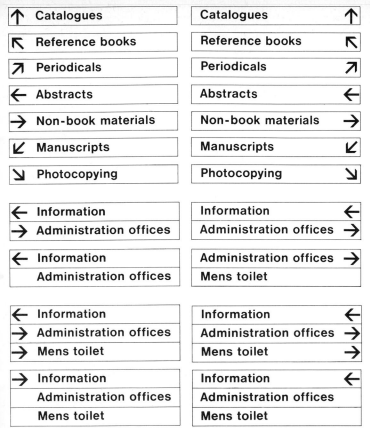

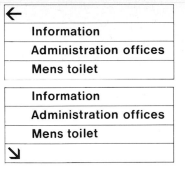

↑	Catalogues
↖	Reference books
↗	Periodicals
←	Abstracts
→	Non-book materials
↙	Manuscripts
↘	Photocopying

Catalogues	↑
Reference books	↖
Periodicals	↗
Abstracts	←
Non-book materials	→
Manuscripts	↙
Photocopying	↘

←	Information
	Administration offices
	Mens toilet

	Information	←
	Administration offices	
	Mens toilet	

←	Information
	Administration offices
	Mens toilet
↘	

	Information	←
	Administration offices	
	Mens toilet	
		↘

| ← | Information |
| → | Administration offices |

| Information | ← |
| Administration offices | → |

| ← | Information |
| | Administration offices |

| Administration offices | → |
| Mens toilet | |

←	Information
→	Administration offices
→	Mens toilet

Information	←
Administration offices	→
Mens toilet	→

→	Information
	Administration offices
	Mens toilet

Information	←
Administration offices	
Mens toilet	

If all arrows are placed either on the left or on the right, then the destination names are always ranged left regardless of the direction in which the arrows are pointing. Note also that the standard panel length is slightly less than that required when the staggered arrangement is used.

three arrangements in terms of their effectiveness, but for aesthetic reasons the staggered arrangement is often preferred. The arrows will then always be pointing away from the destination names, whereas if all of the arrows are placed on the left, for example, arrows pointing to the right will be pointing into the destination names.

If the staggered arrangement is chosen, it may sometimes be appropriate for destination names to be ranged right rather than ranged left. This will be the case with signs consisting of only one or two panels. With three or more panels, however, all of the names should be ranged left to promote rapid scanning.

If all of the destinations on a sign are in the same direction, it is unnecessary to include an arrow on every panel. The arrow can either be placed on a separate panel above or below the destination names, or it can be given beside one of the names. If the arrow is given on a separate panel, the overall length of the panels should not be reduced.

Identification signs

Primary identification signs and labels on storage units present no serious problems in terms of information layout since they generally carry a single destination name. There is no real reason why destination names should not be centred on identification panels if this arrangement is preferred, but ranged-left names will be more in keeping with the rest of the system (if our recommendations are followed) and they will be quicker and easier to produce.

Door signs are a form of identification sign which can be treated in several ways, as shown here. The room number and descriptive word or phrase may appear together in a single line of wording, or the descriptive information may appear on a second line or even on a separate panel. In some situations the depth of the descriptive panel may need to vary in order to accommodate more than one line of lettering where necessary. The length of the panels can either be based on the length of the longest line, or it can be varied according to the length of the wording. It is often convenient to choose two or three standard lengths and to use these as appropriate. If the room number is on a separate panel, this should be the same length as the descriptive panel.

Tier and shelf labels should ideally be in the form of a continuous strip which runs the length of the tier or shelf. The wording should always be ranged left rather than being centred or ranged right. The divisions between tiers are not always obvious, and the position of the lettering can provide a valuable cue. If it is necessary to give two subject headings, these should both be ranged left and linked by punctuation or the word 'and'.

The layout of information on book labels should follow a standard pattern. All labels should be of the same depth, and this will be determined by the length of the longest class-

Information

Information

Information

Information

Information

Information

124	Staff only

504	Cataloguing department

506	Photographic unit Knock before you enter

124

Staff only

504

Cataloguing department

506

Photographic unit

Knock before you enter

mark. If possible, the width of the label should be varied according to the width of the book so that it just reaches the edges of the spine. Alternatively, two or three standard label widths may be used as appropriate.

Information signs

Information signs may carry only a short phrase or sentence, or the message may be long enough and complex enough to be split into paragraphs and to require headings and subheadings.

Paragraphs should always be separated by the use of additional space. Indentation of the first line of each paragraph will then be unnecessary.

Headings should be clearly distinguished from the accompanying text, and it is important that different levels of heading should be immediately recognisable. These distinctions can be made by the positioning of the headings

Left: *Alternative layouts for primary identification signs.*
Right: *Two alternative treatments for door signs.*

53

OVERNIGHT LOANS

**Books may be borrowed
overnight from 1900 hours.
They must be returned by
1030 hours the following
day**

OVERNIGHT LOANS

**Books may be borrowed
overnight from 1900 hours.
They must be returned by
1030 hours the following
day**

**OVERNIGHT
LOANS**

**Books may be borrowed
overnight from 1900 hours.
They must be returned by
1030 hours the following
day**

**OVERNIGHT
LOANS**

**Books may be borrowed
overnight from 1900 hours.
They must be returned by
1030 hours the following
day**

alone, but where possible it is helpful to emphasise headings and to show their relative importance by the use of bolder and/or larger lettering. Once chosen, the layout and typographic style of headings should be consistent on all signs of a similar kind, or the significance of the visual distinctions will be much diluted and readers may be confused.

Instruction signs

Instructions will generally need to be given point by point rather than as continuous text. Additional line spacing should be used between each point in order to differentiate successive stages clearly and to give the information a more open and less daunting appearance. In some cases it may be appropriate to use illustrations or diagrams as well as or instead of text.

Four alternative layouts for information with a single level of heading. There is little difference between these layouts in terms of their effectiveness, but the choice will influence the size and shape of the panel. Note that the space between the heading and text is always greater than the line spacing. The headings could be further emphasised by the use of bold, or a larger type size if there is no bolder weight available in the selected type face. With stencilled lettering, either capitals or a larger stencil could be used for emphasis.

Loans

Overnight loans

Books may be borrowed
overnight from 1900 hours.
They must be returned by
1030 hours the following
day

Restricted loans

These books are issued
for three hour periods.
Please return them after
use

*Three alternative layouts for information with
two levels of heading. The variations in type
size and weight help to make the structure of
the information clear. With stencilled lettering,
it would be advisable to use larger stencils or
capitals to emphasise headings. Again, it is
important to note the effect of the choice of
layout on the size and shape of the panel.*

Loans

Overnight loans

Books may be borrowed
overnight from 1900 hours.
They must be returned by
1030 hours the following
day

Restricted loans

These books are issued
for three hour periods.
Please return them after
use

55

Loans

Overnight loans

Books may be borrowed
overnight from 1900 hours.
They must be returned by
1030 hours the following
day

Restricted loans

These books are issued
for three hour periods.
Please return them after
use

The layout of illustrated instructions using direct labelling.

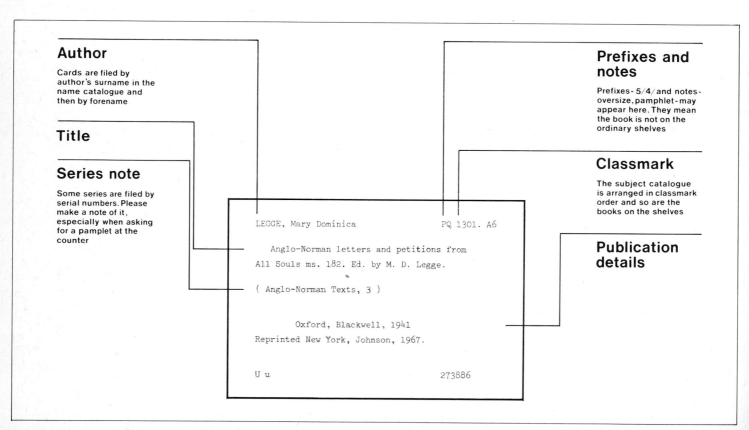

Author

Cards are filed by author's surname in the name catalogue and then by forename

Title

Series note

Some series are filed by serial numbers. Please make a note of it, especially when asking for a pamplet at the counter

Prefixes and notes

Prefixes - 5/4/ and notes - oversize, pamphlet - may appear here. They mean the book is not on the ordinary shelves

Classmark

The subject catalogue is arranged in classmark order and so are the books on the shelves

Publication details

```
LEGGE, Mary Dominica              PQ 1301. A6

    Anglo-Norman letters and petitions from
All Souls ms. 182. Ed. by M. D. Legge.

( Anglo-Norman Texts, 3 )


      Oxford, Blackwell, 1941
Reprinted New York, Johnson, 1967.


U u                                  273886
```

Instead of direct labelling, a numbered key may be used. This often results in a more pleasing layout and a smaller panel. Numbered keys are often essential for more complex illustrations.

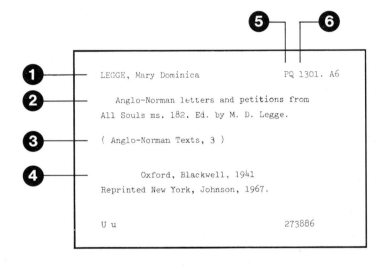

1 Author

Cards are filed by author's surname in the name catalogue and then by forename

2 Title

3 Series note

Some series are filed by serial numbers. Please make a note of it, especially when asking for a pamplet at the counter

4 Publication details

5 Prefixes and notes

Prefixes - 5/4/ and notes - oversize, pamphlet - may appear here. They mean the book is not on the ordinary shelves

6 Classmark

The subject catalogue is arranged in classmark order and so are the books on the shelves

LEGGE, Mary Dominica   PQ 1301. A6

    Anglo-Norman letters and petitions from
All Souls ms. 182. Ed. by M. D. Legge.

(Anglo-Norman Texts, 3)

        Oxford, Blackwell, 1941
Reprinted New York, Johnson, 1967.

U u   273886

Colour

Negative versus positive images

For the reading of continuous printed text it has been shown that dark type on a light background (a positive image) is more legible than light type on a dark background (a negative image). The legibility of messages as short as those typically displayed on signs is unlikely to be affected however, especially if certain precautions are taken.

When a bright image is displayed on a dark background, a phenomenon known as irradiation occurs whereby the borders of the bright image are apparently extended. This means that when light type is displayed on a dark background there will be a tendency for the counters to appear to fill in and for adjacent letters to appear to run together. These tendencies will be counteracted by the use of a type face with large open counters, by the use of a type size which is appropriate for the reading distance, and by the avoidance of tight letter spacing.

The final choice of negative or positive image is likely to depend on the environment in which the signs are to be placed and whether they are required to blend with or stand out from their surroundings.

Colour and legibility

Colours are defined in terms of three variables. These are hue (or wavelength), saturation (or purity of wavelength) and brightness (or physical intensity).

When coloured lettering or backgrounds are used on signs, it is the contrast between the brightness of the lettering and the brightness of the background that is important from the point of view of legibility. Hue and saturation are unimportant, except in so far as they affect contrast. The level of contrast should always be at least 70 per cent for good legibility at a distance, which means that either the lettering must be very dark and the background very light or vice versa.

Uses of colour

Harmony In some situations it will be preferable to choose a single colour scheme for all signs which will harmonise well with the environment. In older buildings, for example, a scheme based on a single combination of relatively subdued colours will often be most in keeping with the surroundings. Combinations such as white or an off-white colour on a dark brown, grey, green, blue etc will be ideal in this situation. Alternatively, the colour of the signs may be chosen to blend with or stand out against the colour of the library decor.

Emphasis If no serious constraints are imposed

by the environment, then colour can be used to distinguish between different kinds and levels of sign or to emphasise individual signs within a group. For example, a distinction might be made between direction-finding signs, information signs and instruction signs. It is important, however, that the different groups of signs should still have a common theme in terms of colour. This could be achieved by using light lettering on a dark background and varying the colour of the background, or by using dark lettering on a light background and varying the colour of the lettering.

Alternatively, all signs might be the same colour except for, say, certain mandatory information signs. These could be emphasised by reversing the direction of contrast (the direction of contrast which will give the most emphasis will depend on the surroundings) or by using a different colour for the lettering or background as appropriate.

Coding Colour can also be used as a means of distinguishing between different geographical areas of the library (for example, different floors, rooms etc), *or* as a means of coding the stock according to subject matter, bibliographical form, reference versus loan collections etc. In this case, all signs in a given area of the library or all signs relating to a particular sub-section of the stock, will be the same colour regardless of the sign group to which they belong. If colour is used in this way, however, the concept of

harmony with the surroundings must be abandoned, and reversal of contrast will be the only way of providing emphasis between or within groups of signs.

In order to be successful, a colour coding system must be simple. It must attempt to code one variable only, and the total number of categories should be limited to eight at the very most. This is the maximum number of colours which the average user is likely to be able to absolutely identify in situations where the complete set is not available for reference.

Colour coding should always be redundant, that is, it should always be used in addition to wording rather than instead of it. Some users may be unfamiliar with the concept of colour coding and may not attach any significance to it initially, and it must also be remembered that 8 per cent of men and 0.45 per cent of women suffer from some form of colour vision defect. In situations where it is not possible or desirable to use words as well as colour (for example on small labels used to colour-code books), an explanation should be provided nearby.

As suggested above, either the sign background or the lettering should vary in colour but not both. Variations in background colour will be more effective because the area of colour will be greater. The colours chosen should be as different as possible in hue, but as similar as possible in brightness. For white lettering on a darker background, a range of strong pure colours giving good contrast should be chosen.

In this situation it will not be possible to achieve maximum contrast because very dark colours can be difficult to discriminate from one another, particularly in poorly lit areas. If black lettering is used, then a range of light, bright colours with a high degree of saturation should be chosen.

Before making a final choice of colours, it is also important to take into account any local regulations relating to the colour of warning and danger signs, as these may restrict the choice of colours available for use in the coding system. It is also worthwhile attempting to choose colours which are easily and unambiguously nameable, so that users can be instructed to follow signs of a particular colour without any risk of confusion.

The exact colours to be used should be selected from one of the standard colour specification schemes available (such as the Munsell system). Care should be taken in choosing colours from small swatches, however, as a small area of colour will often appear to be brighter than a larger area of the same colour. If the signs are to be manufactured by more than one method, great care should be taken in colour matching the various materials used or confusion may result. The materials should not be liable to fading nor should they attract dirt and dust, otherwise any new or replacement signs put up at a later date will differ markedly from the originals and may be interpreted as being a different colour.

Either a negative or a positive image may be used on signs. Whichever direction of contrast is chosen as the standard, the other may be used for emphasis. A white image on a dark background is preferable where colour coding is used however. Black and white are good basic colours for signing, though brown and white will be less stark and may harmonise better with the library decor. Green and orange are examples of colours which are useful for emphasis in systems where the majority of signs are black and white. Strong, pure colours such as green, orange and blue are ideal for colour coding.

Library

Library

Sign placement

Signs should be placed so that they can be seen and read in good time for any necessary action to be taken. This means that they should be directly facing the user as he approaches them, and their height should be such that they are as close as possible to the natural line of vision. Ideally, all signs of a given kind should be placed in a similar position and at a similar height. This reduces the competition between different kinds of sign, because users will eventually learn where to expect to see particular kinds of information.

There are four main ways of fixing signs to the fabric of the building. They may be flat-fixed or projecting from a vertical surface, they may be suspended from the ceiling, or they may be free-standing. Although it is desirable that all signs of the same kind should be fixed in the same way, the physical characteristics of the building may prevent this in some instances and exceptions will therefore need to be made. Often, for example, there is no suitable vertical surface where a sign is needed, and it may then be necessary to consider using a suspended or free-standing sign. Similarly, the ceiling at a particular point may be too high or too weak for a suspended sign, and it will then be necessary to use a wall-mounted or free-standing sign instead.

62

Plans Plans may be flat-fixed if there is a suitable vertical surface, or free-standing. Free-standing plans may be displayed vertically, horizontally or at an angle. The vertically displayed plan is perhaps more likely to attract the user's attention and it can be viewed by several people at a time. The horizontal plan may make it easier for the user to orient himself, but his view of it is easily obstructed by other people. A plan displayed at an angle is likely to have the advantages of both horizontal and vertical displays, without the disadvantages of either. The choice of display angle will affect the display height and the panel size.

Directories Directories will usually be either flat-fixed or free-standing. Their depth will generally be too great for them to be suspended.

The main directory may be flat-fixed if there is a suitable wall or pillar available, or it may be free-standing. In a large entrance hall, a free-standing sign may be necessary in order to bring the directory close enough to the entrance. The sign can then be positioned in such a way

Suitable heights for signs. Projecting and suspended signs should be well out of reach, and flat-fixed signs should ideally be at eye level.

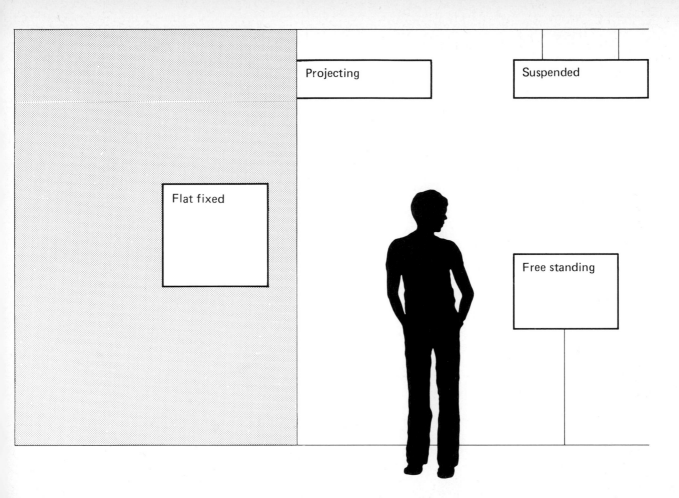

Flat fixed

Projecting

Suspended

Free standing

that it cannot be missed by users entering the library. Sub-directories on other floors are usually best flat-fixed.

Directional signs Directional signs will usually be flat-fixed, projecting or suspended. Free-standing signs are sometimes useful on a temporary basis however.

It is particularly important that directional signs should be positioned so that they are facing the user as he approaches them. Signs in other positions may easily be ignored. A suspended sign is often the best or indeed the only way of placing the information directly ahead of the user, and such a sign will also have the advantage of being visible from a distance. A flat-fixed sign will be appropriate where there is a wall or pillar directly in the user's path, as at a T-junction in a corridor for example. Flat-fixed signs should not be placed on doors however. If the door is wedged open, either the arrow will point in the wrong direction or the sign will be obscured on the back of the door. Projecting signs will sometimes be useful in situations where there is no suitable place to attach a suspended or flat-fixed sign.

With all directional signs it is important to check that the meaning of the arrows is unambiguous when the sign is in position. Arrows pointing left or right rarely give rise to confusion, and an upward pointing arrow is usually assumed to mean 'straight on'. Diagonal arrows are generally used in relation to escalators and staircases, but occasionally it is necessary to use them to imply diagonal movement in a horizontal plane. In this case it is important to ensure that there is no staircase or escalator nearby which the user might ascend or descend by mistake.

Identification signs Identification signs will usually be suspended, flat-fixed or projecting, though in some cases a free-standing sign may be suitable.

Primary identification signs may be suspended over entrances or flat-fixed above or beside them. They should not be flat-fixed across double doors, because if one or both doors are open the message will be partly or wholly obscured. Signs identifying secondary destinations may be suspended over the appropriate area, flat-fixed above, beside or on doors, or projecting above or beside doors. The choice of flat-fixed or projecting signs will depend on the users' line of approach. In some cases it will be appropriate

Placement of signs at a 'crossroads', at a T-junction and in a situation where a corridor leads into an open space. 1, 4 and 8 are suspended signs, 2, 5 and 9 are projecting, 3, 6 and 7 are flat-fixed and 10 is free standing.

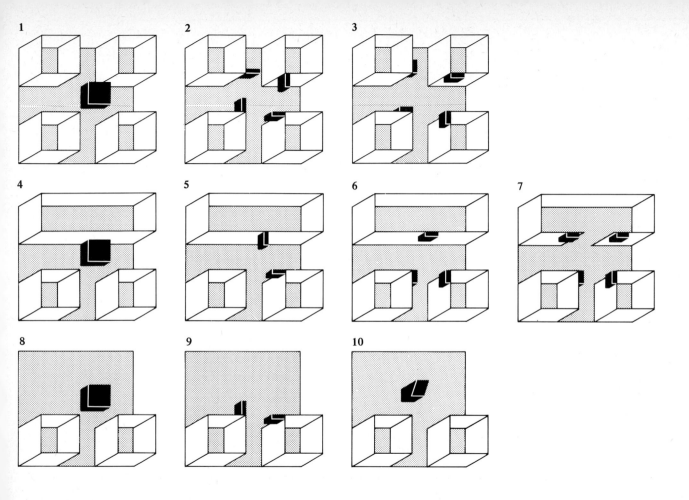

to use both, for example on the ends of book stacks.

Signs on doors leading to offices and areas to which the public does not have access will usually be flat-fixed, and they should be placed in exactly the same position on each door wherever possible. They should be at eye level, and preferably a few inches in from the free edge of the door rather than being centred. If the door has a window or some other obstruction at eye level, the sign should be placed as close as possible to eye level, either above or below the obstruction. This position should then be used consistently on all doors of that type.

If tier and shelf labels of a standard length (as opposed to a continuous strip) are used, they should always be ranged left rather than being centred or ranged right on the tier or shelf. If a tier or shelf includes several subjects, these should be listed on a single label on the left rather than on several scattered labels.

Great care should be taken with the positioning of book labels. Ideally they should all be placed at the same height above the lower edge of the spine. Exceptions should only be made in situations where vital information would be obscured by placing the label in the standard position.

Information signs These may be suspended, flat-fixed, or free-standing on the floor or on a counter or desk. Impact is often an important consideration with information signs, and the method of fixing may need to be chosen with this in mind.

Instruction signs In most cases these are likely to be flat-fixed or possibly free-standing on a desk or counter. They should be placed in such a way that they can easily be read from the point of use of the materials, service or equipment to which they refer. This is particularly important in relation to instructions for using equipment. The user should be able to read them easily from the position he needs to adopt in order to operate the equipment. Thus if he is seated at a microfiche reader, he should not have to stand up in order to read the instructions.

Chapter three **Materials and methods**

In this Chapter we describe some of the basic materials and methods available for sign manufacture. In many cases we have commented on specific products. This is not intended to be a comprehensive survey, however, but rather to give examples of the different kinds of product currently on the market. Where possible we have chosen examples which we feel are likely to give a professional-looking result. With products for in-house sign production, we have also considered the need for materials and equipment to be easy for non-designers to use.

The information given on specific products was, to the best of our knowledge, correct at the time of going to press. Manufacturers are continually improving and broadening the scope of their products, however, so we suggest that they should be contacted direct to confirm details of any items of particular interest.

Choice of materials

In choosing materials and methods for sign manufacture there are several important factors to be borne in mind.

In many cases there will be a limiting factor of cost, which will dictate a choice of materials and methods within a certain price range. It must be realised, however, that the appearance, durability and flexibility of the completed system will depend very much on the quality of the materials used. If it is worth installing a system at all, it is worth installing an attractive system which will last and which will meet the changing needs of the library. The use of unsuitable materials, simply because they are the cheapest available, is a false economy.

In the interests of economy, it is important to consider carefully the degree of permanence required for each group of signs. It would be unnecessarily extravagant to use expensive materials and methods suitable for permanent signs in the production of temporary items. Conversely, materials and methods which are ideal for temporary signs are often totally unsuitable for permanent signs. Materials for permanent signs should be resistant to fading and dirt. They should also be easy to clean, and if outdoors they should be weatherproof and ideally vandalproof too.

The degree of flexibility required is also a very significant factor. Permanent signs need not necessarily be inflexible, provided that a suitable

67

system of panelling and fixings is chosen. If a sign is likely to be replaced or moved in time, the method of fixing should not leave permanent marks on walls or furniture. Temporary signs are of course flexible by their very nature.

The various materials and methods selected must be coordinated as far as possible in terms of colour, type face, type sizes etc. If the signs are to be produced in-house, it is also important to take into account the level of skill and any equipment or facilities required in the use of particular materials and methods. The weight of the panel material may also be important, especially in relation to suspended signs.

In-house sign production

Lettering methods

Typewriters Typewritten text from a standard typewriter is too small for use in a signing system and the quality is not good enough to withstand substantial enlargement. There are, however, typewriters available which produce lettering with a capital letter height of 4 or 5mm.

A type face known as Orator is available for IBM golfball typewriters, and the font includes large and small capitals plus numerals and certain special characters. The Olympia Display face is available in both upper and lower case on a bar typewriter. IBM's Bulletin typewriter also has

upper and lower case characters. Unfortunately this model is no longer manufactured, but it may be possible to obtain one second hand.

These large typewriter faces are suitable for labelling books, pamphlet boxes etc, and also for

Large typewriter faces (same size)

IBM Orator

ABCDEFGHIJKLMNOPQRSTUV
WXYZABCDEFGHIJKLMNOPQR
STUVWXYZ1234567890

Olympia Display

ABCDEFGHIJKLMNOPQRSTUV
WXYZabcdefghijklmnopqr
stuvwxyz12345678910

IBM Directory

ABCDEFGHIJKLMNOPQR
STUVWXYZ abcdefghijklm
nopqrstuvwxyz1234567890

68

temporary information and instruction signs.

IBM United Kingdom Limited
Olympia Business Machines Company Limited

Stencils If stencilled lettering is carefully executed using good quality equipment, it can be both legible and pleasing in appearance.

Several companies manufacture stencils designed to produce lettering which conforms with recommendations made by the International Standards Organisation. Each stencil carries upper and lower case lettering, numerals and certain special characters. Standard sizes range from a capital letter height of 2.5mm to 20 or 25mm. These stencils are intended for use with technical drawing pens made by the same manufacturers. Nibs for these pens are available in a variety of sizes, and it is important to use the correct nib size with each stencil in order to obtain a line thickness which will be appropriate for the letter size.

With good quality stencils designed for ink work, the under surface of the stencil is never in contact with the artwork during use. This prevents ink from spreading under the stencil. The surface is raised by means of edging strips, or by means of a Z-shaped cross-section which allows the lower half of the stencil to rest on the artwork when the upper half is in use, and vice versa.

Uno also supply a range of stencils for display lettering in upper case only. These are available in capital letter heights ranging from 10mm to 100mm. They are designed to provide an outline image in pencil which can be filled in subsequently with ink or felt-tipped pen. Filling-in may be easier if the outline is drawn in ink or felt-tipped pen initially however. If ink is used, it will be necessary to raise the stencil away from the surface of the artwork to prevent ink-

A selection of stencils

spread. This can be achieved by attaching strips of masking tape to the under side of the stencil.

A West and Partners Limited *Uno*
Hartley Reece and Company *Rotring*
Staedtler (UK) Limited

Dry-transfer lettering This kind of lettering is invaluable in the production of both finished signs and artwork for signs or publications. Properly used, it will give results of a professional standard.

Dry-transfer letters are either photographic or printed images which are temporarily affixed to the lower surface of a carrier sheet. A protective backing sheet is also provided, though this is not fixed to the carrier sheet in any way. The images are transferred from the carrier sheet to

Dry-transfer lettering

Dry-transfer lettering produced in-house

the chosen base material by pressure. They adhere best to smooth paper and other similar surfaces.

A very wide variety of type faces is available, and sizes range from 6 point (1.7mm capital letter height) to as much as 192 point (53.5mm capital letter height). Black and white are standard, but some brands are available in colours too. The lettering is sold in sheets, each sheet carrying multiple images of one or more characters. The need to buy whole sheets of lettering, regardless of how many images are actually required, can sometimes be a disadvantage. Some manufacturers supply quarter sheets, however, and these are very useful for small quantities of lettering and for infrequently used characters.

For special requirements which are not met by any of the ready-made products, it is possible to produce dry-transfer lettering in-house using the Letraset Image and Transfer system or the Autotype Artsystem. In-house production is an ideal solution for standard symbols which are not already available in the required sizes, and for special symbols and logotypes. It is also invaluable as a means of producing frequently used words, since the letter spacing and alignment on the carrier sheet will be correct and the whole word can be rubbed down without moving the carrier sheet. The quality of the images is high, and both manufacturers provide a range of colours. The letters are slightly more adhesive than other forms of dry-transfer

lettering and can be used on plastic and glass as well as on paper surfaces.

Both Letraset and Mecanorma will also supply custom-made 'specials'.

Letraset UK Limited
Graphic Systems International   *Rapitype*
Chartpak Europe
Mecanorma Limited
Pelltech Limited   *Alfac*
Autotype International Limited   *Artsystem*

Self-adhesive sign lettering   Self-adhesive sign lettering is ideal for outdoor use since it will adhere to any clean, smooth surface and it is waterproof. It can therefore be wiped over when necessary and it will withstand the elements. It is also ideal for the larger indoor signs.

The letters are either die-cut from thin, flexible PVC, or they are printed. They are produced separately, each on its own individual carrier sheet, and they are usually sold in packs of five. A variety of type faces is available, in capital letter heights ranging from 15 to 150mm. Black and white are standard, but some manufacturers also produce coloured lettering. The products suggested here are among those which provide a simple means of aligning the letters horizontally and of achieving correct letter spacing. Other products without these aids are available, but they are not recommended. Considerable skill is needed in placing

71

letters correctly without any form of guidance, and there is little point in making the task more difficult than it need be.

Letraset UK Limited *Letrasign*
Chartpak Europe
Mecanorma *Normasign*

Self-adhesive sign letters

Photo-lettering machines The Typrinter is a lightweight and relatively inexpensive photo-setting device which can be used in normal room lighting to produce single lines of type. The characters are held on a sheet of film and exposed onto a strip of photo-sensitive paper using ultraviolet light.

Upper and lower case letters, numerals and certain special characters are available for a variety of different type faces (including Helvetica) and in sizes ranging from 18 to 72 point. Letter spacing is under the control of the operator, and is facilitated by an 'instant image' spacing system which shows exactly what has been printed. The resulting lettering is very crisp and can be used in preparing artwork for signs and publications.

The VariTyper Headliner is a rather more sophisticated machine which sets type from plastic discs. A large variety of faces is available in upper and lower case and in sizes varying from 10 to 36 point. Letter spacing is automatic. Some models are capable of setting several lines of type on a single strip of wider paper.

Ashwood Graphics *Typrinter*
VariTyper Corporation *VariTyper Headliner*

Dry-transfer lettering machines The Murotype Kroy 80 produces lettering on self-adhesive tape by a dry-transfer process. Upper and lower case letters, numerals and special characters are held on 80-character type discs. These discs are available for a variety of type faces (including Helvetica and Optima) and in sizes ranging from 8 to 36 point (2 to 9mm capital letter height). Letter alignment and spacing are automatic, and on the whole satisfactory.

Both translucent and opaque tapes are available (the latter in several different colours including white), and they will adhere to a variety of surfaces. This kind of lettering on translucent tape can be useful in the preparation of artwork for signs and publications. On opaque tape it can sometimes be useful for labelling, but unfortunately the tape is rather narrow in relation to the size of the lettering. Labels will need to be protected by a transparent covering of some kind, as the lettering is relatively easily damaged.

Murographics Limited

The 'Typrinter' photo-lettering machine

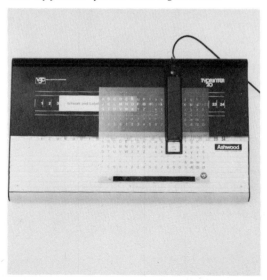

The 'Kroy 80' dry-transfer lettering machine

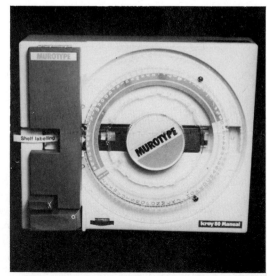

Die-cut lettering machines Murographics Leteron machines are designed to punch out self-adhesive letters from acrylic or paper tapes. The Econosign machine is operated manually, and there is also an Electric Leteron.

Upper and lower case letters, numerals and certain special characters are available for a variety of type faces (including Helvetica), and capital letter heights range from 5/16in to 5in. (The range from 5/16in to 1½in is covered by a single machine, and other models are available which cover the range from 2in upwards.) The letters are automatically aligned and spaced, though with the manual machine the spacing can sometimes be rather erratic if the tape tension is not correct.

Tapes are available in a variety of colours including black and white. Each tape consists of an acrylic or paper layer, sandwiched between a clear carrier sheet and a backing sheet. When the lettering has been punched onto the tape, the carrier is pulled away with the lettering adhering to it. The carrier is then placed in position on the sign surface, and peeled away leaving the lettering in place. The backing sheet will carry a negative image as a result of the removal of the letters, and this too can be used. The backing sheet is removed, and the self-ashesive vinyl or paper tape can then be attached to the desired surface. (The negative is slightly less satisfactory than the positive, however, because the capital letters are centred on the tape. This means that the descenders on lower case letters are rather close to the edge of the tape.)

The lettering will adhere to any smooth, clean surface. The acrylic tapes are suitable for outdoor use and can be wiped clean. The paper tapes are adequate for many indoor applications.

Murographics Limited

The 'Leteron' die-cut lettering machine

74

Panel materials

Mounting board Mounting board of a substantial thickness is suitable for use with dry-transfer lettering, but ideally it should be sandwiched between a firm backing (such as hardboard) and a transparent covering such as perspex. Transparent clips can be purchased to hold the layers together. Mounting board will also be suitable for temporary signs in stencilled lettering, though if the outline of the lettering is drawn in felt-tipped pen, it is wise to use a pen with a fine tip to ensure a sharp outline. A thicker point will allow too much ink to soak into the surface, thus blurring the outline. The alternative is to use artboard. This has a less absorbent surface, but it is more expensive. These materials are available from any graphic arts supplier.

Polystyrene sheet This kind of material is extremely useful for in-house sign production. Bextrene is available in relatively large sheets (1372 x 660mm) and is easy to cut with a Stanley knife. It is available in black and white in thicknesses of up to 1.5mm, and in several colours in a thickness of 0.5mm. The surface will take self-adhesive sign lettering very successfully.

The 0.5mm thickness can be used in label holders or mounted onto a firm backing. Care should be taken in the choice of adhesives, however, as some of them will melt PVC. The 1.5mm thickness will not need mounting in many cases, though with larger signs this may be desirable in order to give them more 'substance'.

GW Film Sales *Bextrene*

Plastic laminates Double-sided melamine, 2mm in thickness, is available in a variety of colours, and it is an ideal base material for self-adhesive sign lettering. It is thick enough and rigid enough not to need mounting, and it is suitable for both internal and external use.

Formica is also suitable for use as panel material, and is available in a wide range of plain colours. Various sizes of sheet are available in a thickness of 1.3mm. The surface will take self-adhesive lettering, and is suitable for both internal and external use. Large signs may need to be mounted on a firm backing with a suitable adhesive.

Techniform Display Limited
Allied Manufacturing Company (London) Limited

Wood-based products Wood-based products which are faced with ply will form a suitable substrate for self-adhesive lettering when painted, and they will result in 'substantial' looking signs. It is also possible to buy wood-based products faced with white melamine. Hardboards, chipboards etc are ideal as backing materials for sign panels which need to be mounted. These products must be well protected if they are used outdoors however.

Moveable lettering systems

Press-fit lettering Moveable lettering is ideal for temporary signs or for information which is changed relatively frequently. There are several systems on the market, but the best-looking is undoubtedly the Modulex system. Each individual letter is on a tile, and the sign panel carries rows of knobs onto which the tiles fit. The lettering is white on a black background and is available in both upper and lower case in a range of sizes. The type face is Helvetica. The tile for each letter is the correct width to ensure good spacing, and the knobs ensure correct alignment. It is also possible to obtain spacing tiles so that the knobbed panel is completely covered and the surface of the sign is flat. The result is a flexible system of signing which is also highly legible and aesthetically pleasing.

WW Instant Signs Limited

Peg lettering Among the most satisfactory peg lettering systems are those in which the pegs on the back of the letter are slid into horizontal grooves on the surface of the panel. Correct letter alignment is therefore automatic, but care is needed with letter spacing. Lettering from the Pintype and Moulded Letter Co is available in a range of sizes in upper and lower case, plus numerals and special characters. The lettering is white or coloured, and the panels are in black. Frames and protective covers are available. Wondersigns Limited also supply this kind of display, but the letters are in upper case only.

With other peg lettering systems, the panel is a pegboard of some kind. Movitex do a range of white lettering on black tiles, and these are pegged into purpose-made black or green panels with relatively inconspicuous perforations. This lettering is available in upper and lower case (plus numerals and special characters) and in a

Modulex press-fit lettering

variety of sizes. Other lettering, not on tiles, is available in large and small capitals, numerals etc, and comes in several sizes. Colours include white, yellow and red. Both alignment and letter spacing are controlled by the perforations in the panel. Frames and a variety of showcases 'glazed' with acrylic material are available.

Peg lettering to fit standard peg boards can also be obtained. Alphapeg and Numapeg are available in black, red, blue and yellow in a range of sizes, but there are no lower case letters.

Pintype and Moulded Letter Company
Wondersigns Limited
Movitex Signs Limited
Librex Educational Company *Alphapeg and Numapeg*

Pin lettering Pin lettering is moulded plastic lettering with pins projecting from the back surface. It can be attached to any reasonably soft surface such as cork or pin board. Upper and lower case letters, numerals etc are available in various sizes and colours. The main problem with this kind of lettering lies in aligning and spacing it correctly. As with magnetic lettering, it is advisable to tape a ruler to the panel to ensure correct alignment. Accidental or deliberate removal of letters may be a problem.

Pintype and Moulded Letter Company
Gaylord Brothers Incorporated

77

Magnetic lettering Magnetic lettering is cut out of a thin rubber material. Alphomag, for example, is a range of sans serif lettering which is available in several sizes in white and other colours. Lower case letters are not available in all sizes however. The magnetic panel is black. Sasco do a similar system with black upper and

Sasco magnetic lettering

lower case lettering on a white panel. The panel can also be written on with felt-tipped pens.

Provided that great care is taken with letter alignment and spacing, magnetic systems can give a neat and pleasing result. It is advisable to tape a ruler to the panel when positioning lettering, in order to ensure correct alignment. The letters are held relatively firmly to the smooth surface of the panel, but ideally they should be protected by a glass or perspex covering to prevent accidental or deliberate interference or removal. If the letters are knocked out of alignment, the appearance of the display will be ruined.

Librex Educational Company   *Alphomag*
Sasco Limited
Philip and Tacey Limited   *Magna-Cel*
Wondersigns Limited

Labelling systems

Labelling of storage units   A variety of label holders for stack, tier and shelf labelling is available. The neatest results are produced when tier and shelf labels can be slid into a continuous channel. Some brands of library furniture include such tracking, or it can be purchased separately and stuck on.

Don Gresswell Limited
Librex Educational Company
Libraco Limited

Balmforth Engineering Limited
Spur Systems International Limited

Stock labelling   Of the labelling methods currently available, the most satisfactory is the Se-lin system. This consists of a Labeler unit which is attached to a typewriter, Se-lin base tape and Se-lin laminating tape. The classmark

Librex shelf-label holder and Spur channelling

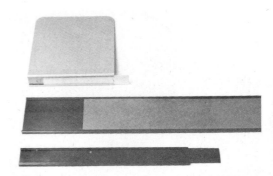

is typed onto the base tape which is then covered with clear laminating tape. After cutting to size, the labels are heat-sealed to the books. If used with a large-face typewriter, highly legible labels can be produced. The tape is available in three widths, and if all the labels are cut to the same depth and placed in the same position on the spine wherever possible, the results can be neat and pleasing as well as highly durable.

An alternative is to use an electric stylus and transfer paper. This is cheaper than the Se-lin system, but can be very untidy in appearance if the lettering is not carefully executed. If a stencil is used, however, neatness and legibility can be greatly improved.

Typed self-adhesive labels can also be used, but unless they are protected in some way they often have a tendency to peel off. They also tend to discolour in time, as a result of the adhesive soaking into the paper.

Librex Educational Company *Electric stylus*
Don Gresswell Limited *Electric stylus*
Gaylord Brothers Incorporated *Se-lin*

Off-the-shelf systems

Dymo The Dymo Modular System consists of a range of panels and a related system of self-adhesive PVC lettering. The lettering can be used on any suitable surface however.

The Dymo panels are of 2mm double-sided melamine in depths ranging from 50 to 400mm. The standard colours are white, yellow, red, green and blue. The panel material is suitable for both internal and external use, and a range of fixings is available.

Dymo modular sign panels

The self-adhesive lettering is made of PVC and comes in black or white. The type face is based on Helvetica, but the letter forms have been slightly modified in order to increase their legibility still further. Upper and lower case letters, numerals and certain special characters are available in capital letter heights ranging from 26.5 to 158mm. Pictograms are also available. The lettering incorporates specially designed systems for letter alignment and letter spacing.

Esselte Dymo Limited

Modulex Modulex manufacture a range of stove enamelled sign panels which are particularly suitable for directional and identification signs. The panels may be single or double sided, and can be wall-mounted, suspended or free-standing. The panel sizes are designed to take lettering of 40, 60, 80 or 100mm capital letter height. Smaller panels for use on doors, desks etc are also available. Standard colours are black, red, blue, green and brown.

The lettering is self-adhesive and white is the standard colour. The type face is Helvetica, and the font includes upper and lower case letters, numerals and special characters. A range of pictograms is also available.

The panels can be supplied with the required lettering already applied, but both panels and lettering are available separately for in-house updating. The panels are not difficult to fix in

position, but the supplier will do this if required.

The Modulex press-fit lettering system described on p76 is visually coordinated with the panels shown here, and can be used to produce a wide range of smaller signs.

WW Instant Signs Limited

Slatz Slatz is a system of interchangeable panelling. The panels are available in 6 different depths and can be cut to the length required. They are made of aluminium, and the standard finish is anodised silver. Colour anodising or stove enamelling can be carried out on request. The panels may be flat-fixed, projecting or suspended. Fixing is by means of a very simple and effective system of clips. Where several panels need to be butted together, they are clipped onto chanelling. The system is very flexible as panels can be moved or replaced in seconds.

Lettering can be engraved, screen printed or photo-etched onto the panel. Alternatively, self-adhesive PVC sign letters can be used in-house.

Spandex UK Limited

Hedway The Syncronol Hedway system consists of a range of stainless steel panels whose sizes are built up from an 80mm module. A variety of fixing methods can be used, and the manufacturer will provide information on these. The lettering is in black and is chemically

The Slatz system

Items from the Modulex range

engraved onto the sign surface by the manufacturer. The type face is Helvetica. Upper and lower case letters, numerals, special characters and a range of pictograms are available. Lettering sizes range from a capital letter height of 10mm to 80mm.

Synchronol Industries Limited

Synchronol Hedway panels

Inventar The Inventar system was designed for the Danish Library Bureau. It consists of aluminium channelling and corresponding panel strips in two depths. These can be cut to any length, and a range of accessories is available for fixing. The signs may be suspended, flat-fixed, projecting or free-standing on desks or tables etc.

The panels which slide into the channelling are normally supplied with black lettering in Helvetica on a white background, but other colours and type faces can be supplied if required. The panels can also be supplied blank.

Don Gresswell Limited

Metalcraft Metalcraft manufacture a range of free-standing, wall-fixed and suspended signs in kit form. Interchangeable panels made of acrylic, aluminium, glassfibre or similar are slotted into aluminium frames. Frames and posts can be anodised or stove-enamelled in British Standard colours. Panels can be supplied in any length, and are available in different thicknesses.

Metalcraft

Interchange aluminium signs This is a system of extruded aluminium panels which are designed to be suspended in banks or flat-fixed. The panels slide onto specially designed fixings, and individual panels can easily be removed, replaced or added to a bank. The panel depth is 100mm, and they can be cut to any length up to 1500mm.

The finish is anodised silver, and lettering is screen printed as required in black or some other dark colour. The planks will accommodate lettering with a capital letter height of up to 55mm.

Bush Signs Limited

Professional sign manufacture

Printed signs

Signs can be printed in a number of ways. Letterpress prints, preferably on a plastic-based paper, can be mounted directly onto sign panels. Photographic prints, also on plastic-based paper, can be treated in the same way. These methods are relatively inexpensive, but they are only suitable for indoor use.

Alternatively, the message may be screen printed onto the surface of the sign. This is an economical production method for permanent signs and it can give very pleasing results. The only disadvantage is that the lettering can be easily scratched with a sharp implement such as a nail or a knife, and this may be a disadvantage for external signs in some situations.

The most durable printed signs are those on which the printing is sub-surface. The lettering can be screen printed onto the reverse side of a thin, transparent vinyl sheet. Background colour is then applied over the image, and the vinyl is bonded to the panel. This method is particularly useful for external signs.

Enamelled signs

Metal signs can be either stove enamelled or vitreous enamelled. An acrylic enamel is generally used in stove enamelling. The panel surface is first covered in the background colour and then baked. The lettering is screen-printed onto the background, and the panel is either baked again or air-dried. Alternatively, decal lettering can be used. This is durable self-adhesive lettering which is cut out of thin metal sheet or vinyl. Stove enamelling is suitable for both interior and exterior use, but it can be easily scratched by vandals.

Vitreous enamel is baked to a much higher temperature than stove enamel, so much so that it can only be used on steel. The lettering is again screen-printed onto the background colour and the complete panel is then baked. The high temperature gives a glass-like weather-proof finish which is resistant to scratching and to vandalism with aerosol sprays. It will chip if heavy objects are hurled at it, but in this situation most other signs would be broken. Vitreous enamelling is relatively expensive however.

Engraved, etched and inscribed signs

All of these processes result in an intaglio image, ie one which is cut or etched out of the surface.

Printed

Enamelled

Etched

Engraving is often carried out on a two-colour laminated plastic. The engraving reveals the second colour beneath, and this forms the image. This method is economical and the results are durable, but not very pleasing in appearance. Because the lettering is mechanically routed, it has a U-shaped cross section and the corners are rounded rather than sharp. The range of type faces and sizes that can be satisfactorily engraved is therefore limited. The method is not suitable for very small signs.

An alternative is to chemically etch the lettering into a metal surface. The image is initially transferred onto the panel by photographic means. The panel is treated with a photosensitive gelatine resist, and the image is exposed onto this surface. The resist hardens in the non-image areas, but can be washed away from the image areas. The panel is then placed in a bath of acid, which etches the unprotected image areas. The resulting intaglio image is usually filled in with enamel. The letter forms are very much sharper than those produced by mechanical engraving, and there is very little limitation on the type faces which can be used. The finished product is very durable and highly professional in appearance, but the method is more expensive than screen printing or engraving.

Lettering can also be inscribed or carved by hand into suitable materials. This requires skilled craftsmanship, and is therefore not a suitable method to use in a large signing system.

It can be very effective for external identification signs however.

Sign-writing

Sign-written lettering is hand painted and can be applied to a wide variety of surfaces. If well executed, sign-writing can be very attractive in appearance. It is a highly skilled craft, however, and only an experienced professional will be able to produce top quality results. For this reason, sign-writing is an expensive method of sign production and it should not be used in situations where printing, etching or enamelling would serve equally well. Its main advantage is that it creates a very distinctive look, and it is therefore often suitable for one-off signs such as external identification signs. It must also be remembered that sign-writing is a highly individual craft, and if a series of related signs begun by one craftsman needs to be finished by another for some reason, the results may not be identical.

Three-dimensional lettering

Three-dimensional lettering can be cast, cut, constructed or moulded. Cast letters are usually made of a metal such as aluminium, or of concrete. Cut-out letters can be of metal, plywood, cork or plastics, and constructed letters are usually of plastic, metal or both. Moulded letters are of plastic.

Signwritten

Three dimensional

All of these methods will create effective three-dimensional lettering which is particularly useful for external identification signs. Cast aluminium or concrete and constructed metal letters are particularly durable and impressive in appearance. Moulded or constructed plastic letters are rather less durable and can be broken if missiles are flung at them.

Fixings for signs produced in-house

The manufacturer or supplier will usually advise on fixings for professionally manufactured and off-the-shelf signs, but fixing methods will need to be found for signs produced in-house. All fixings should be invisible if possible, and they must be chosen according to the degree of permanence required. We suggest a few simple methods here, but with a little ingenuity it will be possible to devise others.

Flat-fixed signs

One of the simplest methods of flat-fixing signs to a vertical surface is to use adhesive pads such as Selotape Sticky Fixers. These will adhere firmly to any smooth, clean surface, yet they can easily be removed with lighter fuel. They are ideal for relatively lightweight signs and for temporary signs.

For a more permanent fixing, a strong adhesive can be used over the whole area of the back of the panel. This method gives no flexibility, however, because it will badly damage the surface to which the sign is stuck.

An alternative is to screw the sign to the wall through its face. This is a very simple and strong method of fixing for permanent signs which will do less damage to the substrate than adhesive, but the screw heads will of course be visible. These should be counter-sunk, unless round headed screws are used. The screw heads should be painted the same colour as the panel and the number of screws should be kept to a minimum.

A more satisfactory method of permanent fixing is to attach keyhole fittings to the back of the panel with adhesive or screws and to slot these over screws on the wall. A cardboard template will be helpful in matching up the positions of the keyholes and screw heads. The heads should fit tightly into the keyholes to prevent the panel from rocking.

For banks of destination-name panels butted together, the total number of screw-holes in the wall can be reduced by the use of battens. This will also mean that if the order of a mixture of single- and double-line panels is changed, thus necessitating new screw holes, the new holes will be made in the batten rather than in the wall. Battens will also make fixing easier on walls with a rough surface.

An invisible fixing to a batten can be achieved by the use of L-shaped brackets, as shown. The

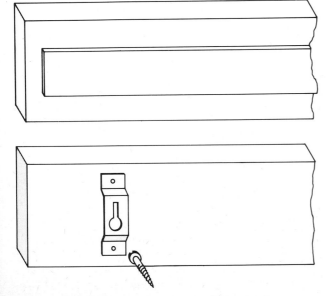

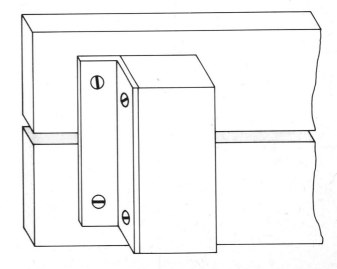

Alternative methods of flat-fixing.

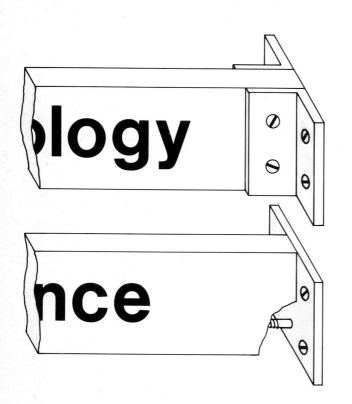

Fixing methods for projecting signs.

The use of keyhole fixings on suspended signs.

bracket is first screwed onto the back of the signs, and then to the batten on the wall. The latter operation will be simpler if corresponding holes are drilled through the bracket and the batten before the batten is fixed to the wall. The bracket can then be screwed to the batten using a long screwdriver. This method is only suitable for relatively thick panels however.

Projecting signs

Projecting panels can be fixed by sandwiching one end between L-shaped brackets and screwing these to the wall. Either adhesive or screws can be used to fix the panel to the brackets, depending on the thickness and weight of the panel. With relatively lightweight panels, an alternative method is to drive screws through a flat plate and into the end of the panel. The plate can then be screwed to the wall. If this method is used, the screws running into the edge of the sign should be staggered rather than vertically aligned, in order to avoid splitting the panel material.

Suspended signs

Sign panels can be suspended on strong nylon thread using eyes screwed into the top edge of the panel and the ceiling. If a bank of two or three hanging signs is necessary, these can be attached to one another using keyhole fixings.

Free-standing signs

These may take a number of forms. Panels may be attached either vertically or at an angle to a stand or legs. Alternatively, a box-like shape can be used. This can either be of such a height that the top surface can be used as a flat or angled sign panel, or it may take the form of a pillar to which direction-finding signs can be flat-fixed.

Chapter four **Design principles in practice**

In Chapter 2 the basic principles of sign design were described in general terms. Here we go on to make specific design recommendations based on these principles. The use of arrows and symbols, the choice of letter sizes and the determination of panel sizes are discussed in relation to four selected type faces. All four faces are suitable for use on signs to be professionally manufactured, and two of them are particularly suitable for use on signs to be produced in-house. Many of the recommendations made in relation to these four faces will also apply to other similar faces.

In order to illustrate the quality of the results which can be achieved by following these recommendations, we have designed and produced two signing systems and photographed them both in context. One of the systems could be produced entirely in-house, while the other would require professional manufacture.

Choice of type face

To illustrate the use of design principles in practice, we have chosen two sans serif faces, Helvetica and Optima, and two seriffed faces, Clarendon and Palatino. Helvetica and Clarendon are particularly suitable for in-house sign production because they are available in a range of sizes of dry-transfer and self-adhesive lettering.

Helvetica Medium was selected as a suitable weight for signing, and equivalent weights were chosen for the other three faces. They were Optima Bold, Clarendon Medium and Palatino Semi Bold.

Helvetica Medium

ABCDEFGHIJKLMN
OPQRSTUVWXYZ
1234567890&?!(.:,;')
abcdefghijklmnop
qrstuvwxyz

Clarendon Medium

ABCDEFGHIJKLMN
OPQRSTUVWXYZ
1234567890&?!(.:,;')
abcdefghijklmnopqr
stuvwxyz

Optima Bold

ABCDEFGHIJKLMN
OPQRSTUVWXYZ
1234567890&?!(.:,;')
abcdefghijklmnop
qrstuvwxyz

Palatino Semi Bold

ABCDEFGHIJKLMN
OPQRSTUVWXYZ
1234567890&?!(.:,;~')
abcdefghijklmnopqr
stuvwxyz

Toilet

2x | Centre

Toilet

2x

Toilet

2x

Toilet

1.5x

Toilet

1.5x

Symbols

As suggested in Chapter 2, the ISO symbols are suitable for use on signs and will harmonise well with both seriffed and sans serif type faces.

The depth of any symbols used should be equivalent to the distance between the top of the ascenders of the lettering to the bottom of the descenders, and they should be centred on the depth of the panel. They should follow any associated wording rather than precede it.

The use of symbols will be restricted to professionally manufactured signs in many cases, because dry-transfer and self-adhesive symbols are not available in a sufficiently wide range of sizes for use on signs produced in-house. It is possible, however, to produce dry-transfer symbols in suitable sizes using Letraset Image and Transfer material or the Autotype Artsystem (see Chapter 3).

The spacing of symbols. (The system of measurement used here is explained on p98.)

92

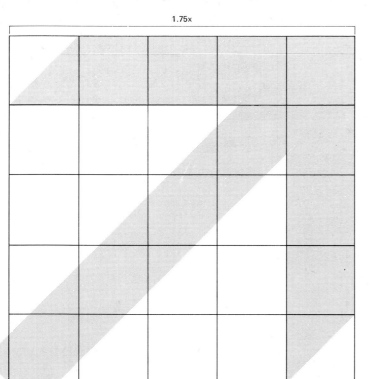

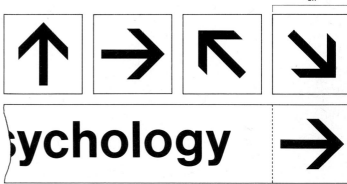

The construction and positioning of the arrow.

Arrows

An arrow of a suitable size and weight to harmonise with all four type faces (and others too) can be constructed very simply on a square grid. The depth of the square is 1.75 times the x-height of the lettering with which the arrow is to be used.

    The arrow is then centred within a square whose size is determined by the panel depth.

Size of lettering

This section is intended to give guidance in the selection of a suitable range of letter sizes. The guidelines given here cannot possibly cover every situation however, and there will be occasions when exceptions will need to be made.

Legibility

It was argued in Chapter 2 that the size of lettering needed for each group of signs depends largely on the maximum distance from which signs in that group will need to be read. In order to give some guidance on the choice of letter sizes for given reading distances, we have carried out distance legibility tests on a range of sizes for each of our four type faces. The results of these tests are shown in the accompanying tables. With care, the data in these tables can be applied to other type faces having a similar style and a similar ratio between their x-height and their capital letter height.

The sizes to be tested were chosen specifically in relation to likely requirements for library signing. (The smaller sizes, for example, were chosen with the restrictions imposed by label holders in mind.) With Helvetica and Clarendon, the choice was also influenced by the sizes available in self-adhesive and dry-transfer lettering. The range of sizes tested for each type face is intended to provide an adequate choice for each group of signs, while at the same time ensuring that an obvious size hierarchy will be created. The reading distances given in the table represent the greatest distance from which our subjects could *comfortably* read single words in each letter size.

To select a letter size from one of the tables, first find the reading distance value which is closest to that required. If the required distance is only slightly greater than one of the tabulated values, the letter size given for that value may be adequate. If, however, the required distance falls midway between two of the tabulated values or is closer to the greater of two values, it will usually be necessary to use the larger of the two letter sizes. Any doubts as to whether a particular size will be large enough should be resolved by carrying out tests on site.

The choice between two alternative letter sizes for a particular group of signs should also be considered in relation to the choices made for other groups of signs. Sometimes it is worth compromising a little on reading distance in order to avoid using a letter size which would be better reserved for some other sign group.

Applicability

The tables on page 96 suggest suitable ranges of sizes for different kinds of signs. The choice of sizes from these recommended ranges will ensure that a meaningful size hierarchy is

94

Table showing comfortable reading distances for a range of capital letter heights (see text).

Helvetica Medium		Optima Bold		Clarendon Medium		Palatino Semi-bold	
Reading distance (m)	Capital height (mm)	Reading distance (m)	Capital height (mm)	Reading distance (m)	Capital height (mm)	Reading distance (m)	Capital height (mm)
1	5	1	5	1	5.2	1	5.5
2	7.9	2	9	1.5	7.9	1.5	9
3.5	15	3	14	3	16.5	3	16
5.5	20	5	20	4	19.8	5	22
7	25	6.5	24	6	25.2	6.5	26
9	30	8	28	9	32.4	8	31
13	38	10	35	11.5	39	10	38
20	50	20	53	19	50.9	20	58
35	75	35	79	35	82	35	89
55	100	55	109	55	110	55	123
85	150	85	162	85	170	85	181

Suggested sizes of lettering for the various sign groups. Note that mandatory and warning information signs may require somewhat larger lettering than other information signs.

	Signs	Helvetica Medium Capital height	Optima Bold Capital height	Clarendon Medium Capital height	Palatino Semi-bold Capital height
External	Direction	50	53	50	58
	Identification	75 100 150	79 109 162	82 110 170	89 123 181
Internal	Direction	30 38	28 35	32 39	31 38
	Directory	5 15 20 25	5 14 20 24	5.2 16.5 19.8 25.5	5.5 16 22 26
	Identification (primary)	30 38 50	28 35 53	32 39 50	31 38 58
	Identification (secondary)	5 7.9 15 20 25	5 9 14 20 24	5.2 7.9 16.5 19.8 25.5	5.5 9 16 22 26
	Mandatory/warning	25 30 38 50	24 28 35 53	25.5 32 39 50	26 31 38 58
	Information	15 20 25	14 20 24	16.5 19.8 25.5	16 22 26
	Instruction	5 7.9	5 9	5.2 7.9	5.5 9

Manufacturers/ suppliers	Helvetica Medium — Capital height										
	5	7.9	15	20	25	30	38	50	75	100	150
Self-adhesive sign letters											
Chartpack				E		E	A	E	E	E	E
Letraset			E		E		E	E	E	E	E
Mecanorma						E		E	E	E	
Murographics			A	A	A			A	A	A	
Dry-transfer letters											
Chartpack	A	A	A	A	A	A		A			
Letraset	E	E	A	A	A	A	A	A			
Mecanorma	A	A	A	A	A	A	A				
Rapitype	E	A	A	E	E	E	A	E			

Manufacturers/ suppliers	Clarendon Medium							
	5.2	7.9	16.5	19.8	25.2	32.4	39	50.9
Self-adhesive sign letters								
Chartpack								
Letraset								
Mecanorma								
Murographics			E					
Dry-transfer letters								
Chartpack	A	A	A					
Letraset	E	E	E	E	E	E	E	E
Mecanorma	A	A	A	A				
Rapitype								

A Approximate size available
E Exact size available

created. It must be emphasised, however, that these tables are intended only as a guide, and individual circumstances may dictate a different solution.

Availability

If the signs are to be professionally manufactured, it will be possible for all four type faces to be reproduced at any size required.

If the signs are to be produced in-house using dry-transfer or self-adhesive lettering, the choice of sizes will be limited to those available from the lettering manufacturers. It may be seen from the table on the facing page that Helvetica is available in a wide range of sizes in both dry-transfer and self-adhesive lettering, but Clarendon is available in dry-transfer lettering only. This means that signs requiring lettering in Clarendon with a capital letter height greater than 50mm would need to be produced photographically or professionally manufactured.

The availability of Helvetica Medium and Clarendon Medium in dry-transfer and self-adhesive lettering.

Panel sizes

As suggested in Chapter 2, it is convenient to use the x-height of the lettering as a unit of measurement for all panel dimensions. In this way it is possible to make general statements which will be true for any size of lettering. Optimum dimensions will sometimes vary according to the type face however. This is explained below.

Directories, directional and identification signs

For all single-line directory and directional panels with lettering in Helvetica, Optima, Clarendon or Palatino, a suitable panel depth will be 3x, or three times the x-height of the chosen letter size. This will give appropriate line spacing when several panels are butted together.

Slightly broader margins are desirable for identification signs however. A minimum panel depth of 3.5x will be suitable for a single-line panel, but even more generous upper and/or lower margins can be used as required, as suggested in Chapter 2. In the case of labels

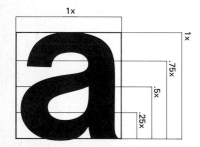

The x-height system of measurement.

98

which are intended to be fitted into holders, the visible panel depth should not be less than 2.5x. The overall panel depth must, of course, fit the label holder.

If the destination name is long enough to need breaking into two lines, simply doubling the panel depth will result in excessive line spacing in relation to the depth of the upper and lower margins. On directory and directional panels in particular, it is important that the space between lines on the same panel should be less than the space between lines on adjacent panels. The correct line spacing in terms of the distance between the base of the x-height on the first line and the base of the x-height on the second line will be as follows:

Helvetica   2.25x
Optima   2.5x
Clarendon   2.5x
Palatino   2.5x

(The value for Helvetica is only 2.25x because this type face has a particularly large x-height in relation to its capital letter height, and a spacing of 2.5x would therefore be too generous.)

To determine the panel length for a particular group of directory, directional or identification panels, it will first be necessary to find out the exact length of the longest line of lettering. This will mean preparing an accurate layout using the correct type face, type size, letter spacing and word spacing (see Chapter 5). If there are several long lines containing almost equal numbers of characters and spaces, it will

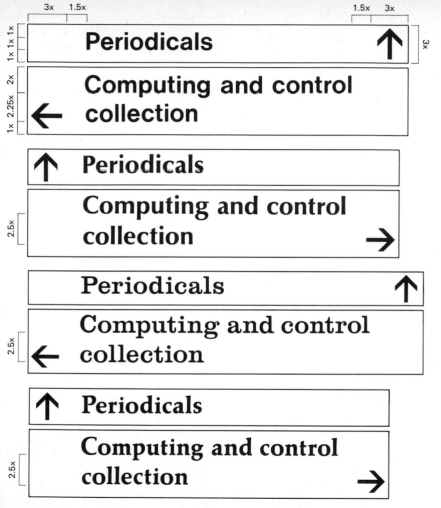

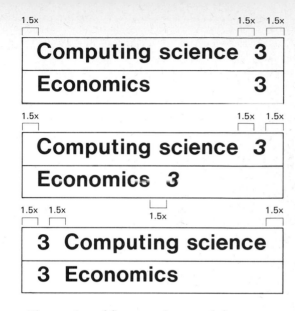

The spacing of floor numbers on alphabetical directories.

Dimensions for directional signs in Helvetica, Optima, Clarendon and Palatino.

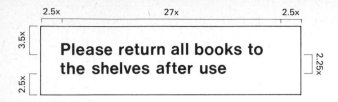

2.5x   **27x**   **2.5x**

3.5x

Please return all books to the shelves after use

2.5x

2.25x

Above: *Dimensions for information panels without headings.*

be necessary to prepare accurate layouts for all of them. Given that letters vary in their width, this is the only satisfactory way of determining which will in fact be the longest line.

A margin of 1.5x should then be added to each end of the longest line. The resulting combination of lettering and margins is the basic unit from which all directory, directional and identification panels are built up.

For floor-by-floor directories and identification signs, the standard panel length will simply be the length of the longest line plus margins. With alphabetical directories and directional panels, however, allowance must be made for floor numbers and arrows respectively.

Information and instruction signs

A suitable line length for information and instruction panels will be 27x. This will result in a maximum of about 30 characters per line, regardless of the letter size used. Allowing for left- and right-hand margins of 2.5x, the total panel width will then be 32x. Consistent use of this system will result in a coordinated series of panel widths which vary in direct proportion to the size of the lettering.

In order to determine the panel depth required for an individual sign or a group of signs, it will be necessary to prepare an accurate layout using the following dimensions.

For panels without headings or with headings in the same type size as the text, the base

Opposite page, top: *Dimensions for panels with headings in the same letter size as the text.* **Centre left:** *Where two signs with messages of different lengths are to be placed side by side, their panel sizes should be the same.* **Bottom:** *Dimensions for panels with headings in a larger size than the text. (Remember that the two-line heading is spaced in terms of its own x-height.)*

(All dimensions shown here will also be correct for Optima, Clarendon and Palatino, except for the line spacing. This should be increased to 2.5x for these three faces.)

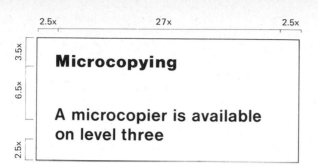

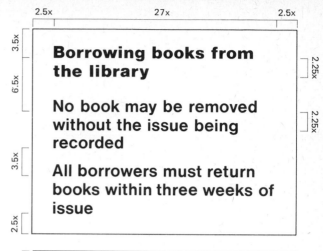

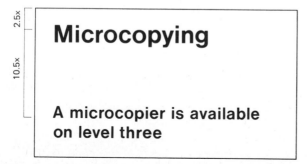

of the x-height on the first line should be 3.5x from the top edge of the panel, thus creating an upper margin. Where there is a heading, the base of the x-height of the first line of text should be 10x from the top of the panel. The line spacing for multiple-line headings and for the text itself should be 2.25x for Helvetica and 2.5x for Optima, Clarendon and Palatino. (Line spacing is measured between the bases of the x-heights on adjacent lines.) The space between paragraphs should be 3.5x for Helvetica and 3.75x for the other three type faces (again measured between the bases of the x-heights). The lower margin should measure 2.5x from the edge of the panel to the base of the x-height on the bottom line, unless a deeper margin is required for coordination with other panels.

If a larger type size is used for the heading, an x-height one and a half times larger than that of the text lettering will be appropriate (ie 1.5x). The top of the x-height of the first line of the heading should then be 2.5x from the top edge of the panel and the base of the x-height of the first line of text should be 13x from the top edge of the panel. Note that these measurements refer to the x-height of the lettering used for the body of the text. All other dimensions will be the same as those given above. If the heading should run to two lines, the spacing between those two lines is best considered in terms of their own x-height rather than that of the text lettering. The standard spacing should be 2.25x for Helvetica

and 2.5x for the other three faces, but if there are no descenders in the first line *and* no capitals or ascenders in the second line, the spacing can be reduced to 2x or 2.25x.

A system suitable for in-house production

External signs The external directional and information signs illustrated here consist of Letrasign self-adhesive sign lettering on melamine panels. The external identification sign is Letrasign lettering applied direct to the fascia of the building.

Internal signs The internal directional signs consist of Normasign self-adhesive sign lettering on melamine panels. Directories, identification signs and information signs are made of melamine or painted plywood with Letrasign lettering. Instruction signs consist of Letraset dry-transfer lettering on thin card, mounted on hardboard. Stack, tier and shelf labels also consist of dry-transfer lettering on thin card, unmounted. All dry-transfer lettering is covered with a protective spray coating.

5

Librarian
Library administrative offices
Cataloguing department
Acquisitions department

4

Tensor Society
Operational Research Society
Library
Life science collection
Mens toilet

3

Periodicals and abstracts
Computing and control collection
Womens toilet

2

Main book collection
Restricted loan collection
Mens toilet (facilities for the disabled)

1

Information
Issue and return counters
Catalogues
Reference books and bibliographies
Micro-readers
Photocopying services
Womens toilet (facilities for the disabled)

4

Tensor Society
Operational Research Society
Library
Life science collection
Mens toilet

Heart pacemakers

There is a security system operating in this library

It is harmless to the general public but may affect a certain type of pacemaker

If you are wearing a pacemaker do not enter the library without contacting an official

Cases and bags

Cases and bags may be taken into the library provided that any books in them are shown on request

No smoking

Issue and return counters →

Information →

Stairs to other levels ←

Womens toilet (facilities for the disabled) ←

Issue and return counters →

Information

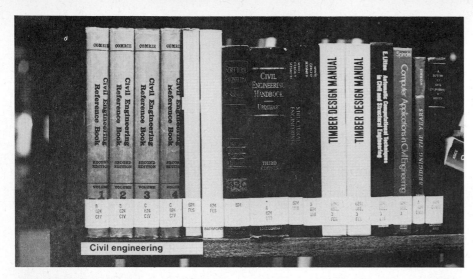

Civil engineering

Using the microfiche catalogue

Inter-library loans

Restricted loan collection

How to find periodicals

124

Staff only

A professionally manufactured system

Signs such as those illustrated in the following photographs could be produced by a number of methods.

External signs External directional and information signs could be anodised aluminium panels with the lettering etched and infilled with enamel, or they could be stove enamelled or screen printed. The external identification sign illustrated here could consist of either moulded or constructed plastic lettering.

Internal signs Ideally the majority of internal signs would be screen printed. Photographic prints on plastic-based paper, though less durable, could be used as an economy measure if necessary. Photographic prints could also be used for temporary signs.

Opening hours

Term Weekdays 9.30am-9.00pm
Saturdays 9.30am-5.30pm
Vacation Weekdays 9.30am-5.30pm

Cases and bags

Cases and bags may be taken into the library provided that any books in them are shown on request

No smoking

5
Librarian
Library administration offices
Cataloguing department
Acquisitions department

4
Tensor Society
Operational Research Society
Library
Life science collection
Toilet ♈

3
Periodicals and abstracts
Computing and control collection
Toilet ♀

2
Main book collection
Restricted loan collection
Toilet ♈ ♿

1
Information
Issue and return counters
Catalogues
Reference books and bibliographies
Micro-readers
Photocopying services
Toilet ♀ ♿

5
Librarian
Library administration offices
Cataloguing department
Acquisitions department

4
Tensor Society
Operational Research Society
Library
Life science collection
Toilet ♈

3
Periodicals and abstracts
Computing and control collection
Toilet ♀

2
Main book collection
Restricted loan collection
Toilet ♈ ♿

1
Information
Issue and return counters
Catalogues
Reference books and bibliographies
Micro-readers
Photocopying services
Toilet ♀ ♿

Heart pacemakers

There is a security system operating in this library

It is harmless to the general public but may affect a certain type of pacemaker

If you are wearing a pacemaker do not enter the library without contacting an official

---

Issue and return counters →
Information →
← Stairs to other levels
← Toilet ♀ ♿

Issue and return counters →
Information

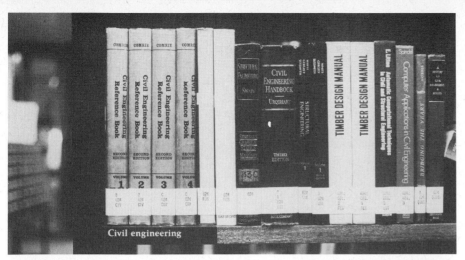

Civil engineering

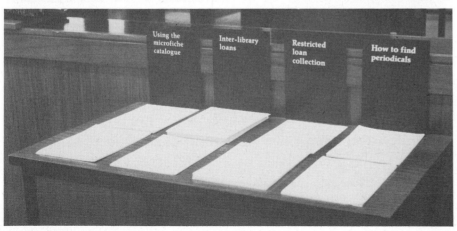

Using the microfiche catalogue

Inter-library loans

Restricted loan collection

How to find periodicals

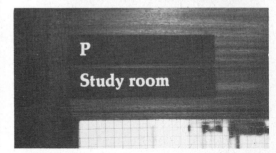

P

Study room

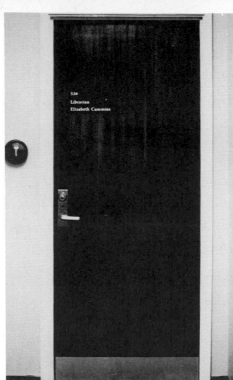

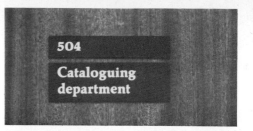

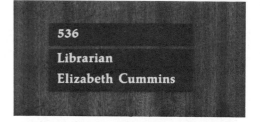

Chapter five **Sign production**

In this Chapter we deal with some of the basic equipment and skills necessary for in-house production, and also with the preparation of specifications and artwork for use by a professional sign manufacturer.

Basic equipment and materials

Certain basic items will be required for sign production and for the preparation of artwork. The importance of buying good quality equipment and materials cannot be over emphasised if a professional result is desired. The necessary expenditure will be more than justified in terms of time saved and frustration avoided.

The largest and most expensive item will be the drawing board. An A2 board, together with a T-square and a set square, will be adequate for most purposes, but the task of sign production will be considerably easier on an A1 board with a parallel motion device (a system of moveable rules fixed to the board). A transparent plastic or perspex ruler will be useful for making measurements, and a 24in metal ruler for use as a cutting edge. For cutting card or mounting board, however, it is worthwhile purchasing a metre rule in heavy metal with a non-slip lower surface. A Stanley knife is an essential item for cutting paper, card or board, and a scalpel will be useful for delicate cutting and lifting operations (in the laying of self-adhesive lettering for example), and for sharpening pencils to a fine point.

A pair of dividers will save much time in drawing guidelines for lettering at constant intervals. An HB graphite pencil will be needed for drawing guidelines directly onto the sign panel material, and a light blue pencil is essential for guidelines on artwork so that the lines will not be reproduced when the artwork is photographed. Pencil lines on sign panels should be removed with a vinyl-plastic eraser. This kind of eraser is less likely to leave grubby streaks than an India rubber eraser. A long soft brush will be needed to brush away dust from the eraser.

A technical drawing pen (such as a Rotring Rapidograph) will be necessary for drawing trim lines on artwork, and for stencilling. The nibs for such pens are hollow tubes through which the ink flows, and they are accurately machined to produce lines of precise widths. The 0.3mm size is suitable for general purpose use, and other

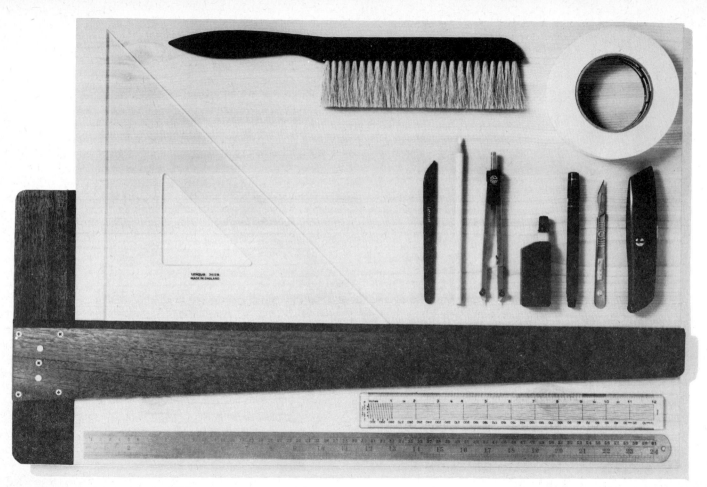

sizes suitable for stencilling can be purchased individually as required. Stencil manufacturers usually suggest suitable line thicknesses for each stencil in the information accompanying the product. The use of a technical drawing pen requires a somewhat different technique from the use of any other kind of pen, but again the manufacturer will supply a leaflet giving advice on the use and care of these pens. They should always be used with inks recommended and/or supplied by the manufacturers, as other kinds of ink will quickly block the narrow channel in the nib.

For the laying of dry-transfer lettering, a purpose-made burnisher is an essential item. The use of any other object for burnishing will often result in cracked or broken letters and possibly marks on the surface of the panel or artwork. Masking tape will be useful for the removal of any misplaced dry-transfer items, and also for fixing the panel material or artwork to the drawing board.

Dry-transfer lettering for sign panels or artwork can be laid on a good quality mounting board. For any form of ink work (other than trim marks), however, it is essential to use a substrate with a chalk-coated surface. This will give crisp ink lines and will tolerate the 'tidying up' of lines or corners by gentle scraping with a scalpel. Examples of suitable surfaces are artboards, such as Daler Superline, or coated papers such as Bristol Board and CS10. Papers and thin boards will need to be mounted if they are

to be used as sign panels. Mounting is also advisable for artwork on such materials in order to give them more rigidity and hence reduce the risk of damage due to folding or creasing.

In-house production

Preparing a 'layout'

Before beginning work on the production of a sign or group of signs, it will be wise—or even essential in some cases—to prepare an accurate layout sheet. With directory, directional and identification panels, a layout sheet will probably only be necessary for the sign in each group with the longest line length, so that the standard panel size for that group can be determined. The same will also be true for relatively simple information and instruction panels, but for more complex panels and for those whose depth will depend on the length of the wording, it is advisable to prepare a layout for each panel. When some experience has been gained in producing signs according to a particular specification, however, it may be possible to dispense with preliminary layouts in most instances.

Layouts should be prepared on paper which is sufficiently transparent to allow tracing. A tracing pad or a 'typo/detail' pad will contain suitable paper. It is advisable to buy an A2 pad and to cut the sheets to size as necessary.

Always work with a sheet of paper which is larger than the estimated size of the panel. For direction-finding panels, begin by drawing a vertical pencil line to mark the boundary of the left-hand margin and a horizontal line on which to position the lettering. For information and instruction signs, two vertical lines will be necessary to define the maximum line length, and a series of horizontal lines the approximate distance apart will be needed for guidance in placing the letters.

The wording should then be traced from dry-transfer or self-adhesive letters of the appropriate size. Care should be taken over the letter and word spacing, and on no account should any word or part of a word be allowed to extend into the right-hand margin. The outline of the lettering may be traced *lightly* in pencil, or alternatively a felt-tipped pen may be used to give solid black letters. It will be much easier to judge the correct letter and word spacing if solid letters are used, but in this case it will be necessary to use typo/detail paper because tracing paper will not accept ink from felt-tipped pens. When the lettering has been traced, the appropriate margins can be added and the panel borders drawn in.

The resulting layout will be a guide to the size of the finished panel, but it may not be exact because it is difficult to judge letter and word spacing correctly when tracing. It may be that when the lettering itself is laid, the true line length for direction-finding signs will be longer or shorter than anticipated. In the case of information and instruction signs, it may be necessary to carry a word over to the next line or to take it back to the end of the previous line, and this could affect the total number of lines required for the message. For this reason, the lettering should always be laid on an area of panel material which is larger than that likely to be needed. The edges can then be trimmed after the lettering has been laid.

Guidelines for lettering should be drawn on the panel material with a *sharp* HB pencil using light pressure. The guidelines needed will be the same as those used on the layout. Care should be taken to protect the surface of the panel from perspiration and grease from the hand while drawing the guidelines, as this may prevent the lettering from adhering properly. If it is necessary to rest the hand on the panel, a spare piece of tracing paper should be used to protect the surface.

It will be found that the system of letter alignment used by some lettering manufacturers is such that the base of the x-height of each letter will fall just above the pencil guideline. This will not matter so long as the guidelines are the correct distance apart (where there is more than one line of lettering) and the position of the panel edges has not been predetermined. When all the lettering has been laid, an allowance for margins can then be added and the panel material trimmed to size.

118

Use of stencils

The first step is to draw appropriate guidelines. It may be helpful to tape a set square or ruler in position on each horizontal guideline as it is used. The stencil can then be slid along the edge of the set square or ruler, thus ensuring perfect alignment of the letters.

A technical drawing pen with a nib of the appropriate thickness should always be used with stencils. Manufacturers of good quality stencils generally provide full instructions for use, and with care and a little practice it is possible to produce acceptable results. It is particularly important to ensure that ink does not flow under the edges of the stencil. This should not happen with good quality stencils, since they are designed to prevent it. It is also important to take care not to smudge freshly drawn lettering when the stencil is moved. Any small areas of ink-spread or smudging can be removed by very gentle scraping with a scalpel. To protect the surface of the panel from being scratched or otherwise damaged by the movement of the stencil over it, a piece of tracing paper should be placed under the ruler or set square in such a way that it projects under the lower part of the stencil too. The stencil will then slide on the tracing paper instead of on the panel surface.

Stencilled lettering should be spaced according to the principles given in Chapter 2.

The appearance of all stencilled lettering will be greatly enhanced if the unavoidable breaks in the letterforms are subsequently filled in. Larger stencilled letters which consist of outlines only will be more legible if the entire letter is carefully filled in, using either Indian ink and a brush or a felt-tipped pen.

The appearance of stencilled lettering will be much enhanced if breaks in the letter shapes are subsequently filled in.

LIBRARY
LIBRARY

Applying dry-transfer lettering

The procedure for applying dry-transfer lettering is as follows (page 121).

1 The first step is to draw pencil guidelines on the base material as necessary. A spare piece of backing paper should be placed over the base material beneath the first horizontal guideline to be used, to prevent unwanted letters from becoming accidentally detached from the carrier sheet. The carrier sheet is then placed over the artwork in such a way that the required letter is correctly positioned.

Correct positioning is relatively easy to achieve with products such as Letraset's which give alignment marks below each letter. If the marks are always carefully positioned on the guideline, all the letters will be upright and at the same level. The marks themselves have a thickness however, and it is important to be consistent in placing the lower edge of each mark on the guideline. (The alignment marks are also intended to assist with letter spacing, but the resultant spacing is too tight for good legibility on signs. Letters should be spaced according to the principles given in Chapter 2.)

2   The area of the carrier sheet immediately over the letter is then burnished gently in all directions to effect the transfer of the letter to the base material. (Large letters should be gently burnished for initial contact before transfer is attempted.)

3   Once the letter has been transferred, the carrier sheet is gently removed. The position of the letter can then be checked, and if it is satisfactory it can be covered with a spare piece of backing paper and burnished firmly. If burnishing is too vigorous, however, or if an instrument other than a burnisher is used, there

is a risk that the letters will become distorted or cracked.

4   If the position of any letter is unsatisfactory, it can easily be removed with a piece of masking tape. The tape is lightly pressed over the letter and then peeled away.

5   When all of the lettering has been laid, remember to erase any pencil lines from the panel material. A piece of backing paper should be placed under the hand to protect the surface of the artwork during this process.

6   Dust from the eraser should be gently removed with a brush. Do not attempt to blow the dust away or to remove it with the hand; these methods are likely to deposit saliva or grease respectively on the panel.

7   If the surface of the panel is not to be protected with a transparent covering of any kind, it should be sprayed with a protective coating. Letraset's Letracote sprays are ideal for this purpose. A first coat should be applied and allowed to dry, followed by a second.

Applying self-adhesive sign lettering

Letrasign and Normasign are examples of self-adhesive lettering which is suitable for use on signs (see Chapter 3). These particular products incorporate a simple spacing system which will give professional results if properly used.

Before attempting to apply self-adhesive lettering, it is advisable to clean the base material with lighter fuel to remove any traces

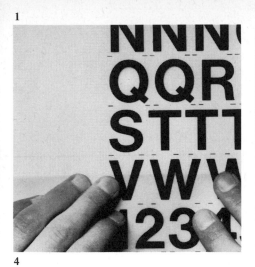

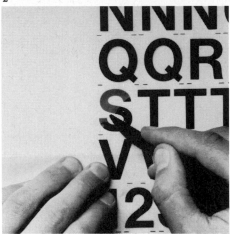

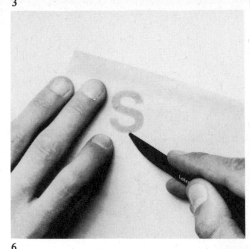

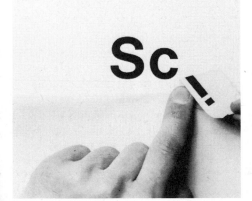

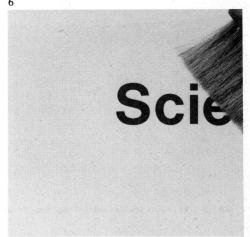

Applying dry-transfer lettering

of grease. A strip of masking tape should then be laid to serve as a horizontal guideline. To ensure that the tape is straight, it should be laid along the edge of a ruler which has been placed across the panel material and taped to the drawing board.

The procedure for laying Letrasign is then as follows (page 123).

1 Each letter is backed by its own carrier sheet which is in two halves. The upper half of the carrier sheet is removed from the first letter. The base of the carrier sheet is then placed on the edge of the masking tape and the upper half of the letter is pressed lightly onto the base material.

2 The upper half of the carrier sheet of the second letter is removed. The base of the carrier sheet is rested against the edge of the masking tape as before, and its left-hand edge is butted up to the right hand edge of the carrier sheet of the first letter. The upper half of the second letter is then pressed down. Further letters are added in the same way.

3 In the case of the letter i, the dot will need to be positioned separately by eye.

4 The lower portion of each carrier sheet is then removed and the lower half of each letter is pressed onto the base material. The letters can then be burnished gently, though they will already be firmly stuck to the panel. A sheet of tracing paper should be used to protect the letters from friction damage during burnishing.

5 When the line of lettering is completed, the masking tape can be gently peeled away.

The procedure for laying Normasign is only slightly different in detail (pages 124-5).

1 Each Normasign letter is sandwiched between an adhesive carrier sheet and a backing sheet. The carrier sheet should be cut back before each letter is used, or it will overlap the previously laid letter. There is then a risk that the letter will be lifted when the adhesive carrier sheet is removed. On no account should the alignment and spacing marks be cut away however.

2 The backing sheet is removed from the first letter.

3 The horizontal alignment marks on the carrier sheet are then placed on the edge of the masking tape and the letter is gently pressed onto the panel surface.

4 The backing sheet is peeled away from the next letter which is then positioned in a similar way. The vertical strokes of the two adjacent alignment marks should overlap.

5 With this kind of lettering, the dot on the i is automatically correctly positioned.

6 Each letter should then be firmly burnished down with a burnisher. Unless this is done, the letters will not adhere properly to the panel surface.

7 The carrier sheets are gently peeled away.

8 The masking tape can then be removed.

1

2

3

4

5

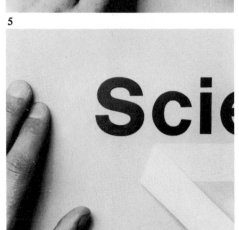

Applying Letrasign self-adhesive sign lettering

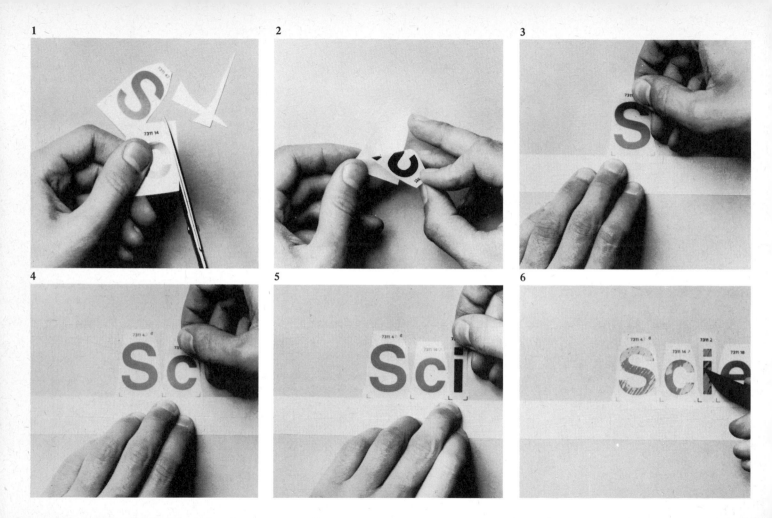

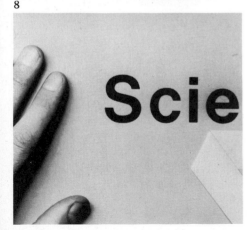

Applying Normasign self-adhesive sign lettering

Professional production

Preparing specifications for the manufacturer

If the signs are to be professionally manufactured, in most cases it will only be necessary to provide the manufacturer with a written specification and layout, rather than with finished artwork.

A written specification should be prepared for each individual sign panel. The sign should be identified by a number, and the specification should give details of the wording, the materials to be used for the sign panel and the lettering, their colours, the type face, the letter size, the dimensions of the panel, the fixing method to be used and the location of the sign. It is important to specify the fixing as this may need to be incorporated by the manufacturer. It is not until a specification of this kind has been produced for each sign required that the manufacturer will be able to give an accurate cost estimate.

The layout should give all the dimensions necessary to enable the manufacturer to position the lettering correctly on the panel, but it need not be full size or exactly to scale. The internal dimensions of the panel should be specified in terms of x-height, as shown in Chapter 4. It will usually only be necessary to produce one layout for each sign group, though an individual layout may be required for any panels differing from the norm.

A written specification or schedule for a series of signs.

Sign No	Wording	Lettering			
		Typeface	Cap height	Colour	Material
B20	2	HELVETICA	100 mm	BLACK	SCREEN PRINTED
B21	MAIN BOOK COLLECTION	"	25 mm	"	"
B22	RESTRICTED LOAN COLLECTION	"	"	"	"
B23	MENS TOILET 🚶	"	" HEIGHT OF SYMBOL: 32MM	"	"
C24	← INFORMATION	"	30 mm DEPTH OF ARROW: 22·5 mm	"	"
C25	ADMINISTRATION OFFICES →	"	"	"	"
C26	PHOTOCOPYING ↓	"	"	"	"
D27	FIRE AND ACCIDENTS SHOULD BE REPORTED AT ONCE TO STAFF AT THE INFORMATION DESK	"	25 mm	"	"

Panels				Quantity	Location
Dimensions	Colour	Material	Fixing		SEE DRAWN SPEC & PLAN
00mm X 000mm	WHITE	¼" THICK PLASTIC	INVISIBLE SCREW	ONE	NEXT TO LIFT ON SECOND FLOOR.
00mm X 000mm	"	"	"	TWO	" " " AND NEXT TO LIFT ON GROUND FLOOR
"	"	"	"	"	" " "
"	"	"	"	"	" " "
00mm X 000mm	"	"	SUSPENDED	ONE	MAIN ENTRANCE. GROUND FLOOR.
"	"	"	"	"	" " "
"	"	"	"	"	" " "
00mm X 000mm	"	"	INVISIBLE SCREW	FIVE	ONE ON EACH FLOOR " " "

Preparing artwork for the manufacturer

For many of the production processes used in sign-making, it is necessary to begin with a high quality artwork image of the wording required for the panel. This is then photographed, and the photographic image is used as a basis for subsequent stages in the process.

Artwork for the manufacturer need not necessarily be full size, but it should not be less than half size. If the recommendations given in Chapter 4 are followed, the correct sign proportions will be obtained when the artwork is enlarged, regardless of the size of lettering used.

A layout should first be prepared, as de-

Information

2

The preparation of artwork for the manufacturer.

1 *An accurate layout is first prepared. The exact position of the panel edges can be determined at this stage in situations where the standard panel size has already been established.*

2 *The artwork is prepared on a piece of mounting board which is large enough to allow generous margins outside the area of the sign itself. Light blue guidelines are drawn in to indicate the position of the lettering and the edges of the panel.*

3

Information

4a

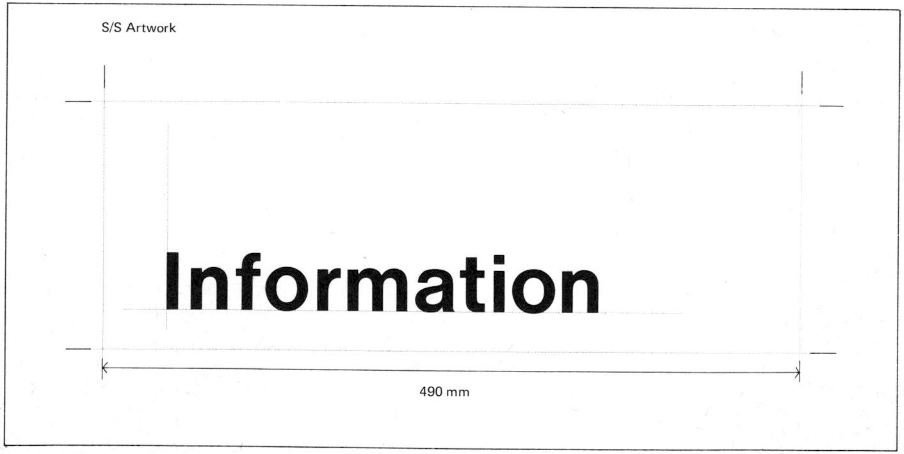

S/S Artwork

Information

490 mm

scribed on p117. A piece of mounting board which is slightly larger than the required size should then be taped to the drawing board with masking tape, and guidelines should be drawn where necessary in light blue pencil.

Dry transfer lettering should then be applied using the method described on p121, except that in the case of artwork it is often more convenient to align the letters by eye and to place them directly on the guideline rather than using the lettering manufacturer's alignment marks. When producing a sign panel it is an advantage for the letters to be positioned slightly above the guideline so that the line can subsequently be erased without any risk of damaging the lettering. On artwork, however, it is not necessary to erase the pale blue pencil lines, and the positioning of the lettering directly on the guideline is helpful in determining the position of the edges of the panel. While applying the lettering it is very important to keep the artwork clean, as any dark stains or smudges may reproduce.

3 *Dry-transfer lettering is laid directly onto the drawn guideline.*
4a *The area of the panel should be indicated by trim marks in ink. If the artwork is full size, this should be indicated as shown. The exact dimension of the longest side should be confirmed.*

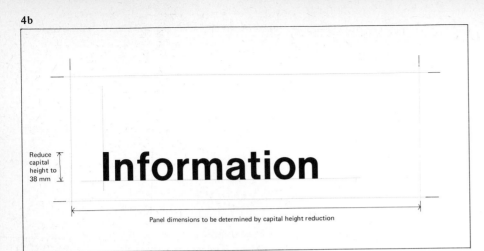

Reduce capital height to 38 mm

Information

Panel dimensions to be determined by capital height reduction

5

Name
Address
Tel No

Trim marks should then be drawn in ink to indicate the position of the edges of the sign. It is essential that these marks should be accurately positioned or the size of the final panel will be incorrect. Any special instructions to the manufacturer should be written clearly and concisely on the edge of the mounting board outside the area of the sign itself. These instructions should include a statement as to whether the lettering is to be dark on a light background or vice versa, and they should give the desired measurement of the longest side of the sign panel after enlargement. The artwork should then be covered with a sheet of tracing paper for protection. The paper can be attached to the back of the mounting board with masking tape.

4b *If the artwork is not full size, the necessary enlargement or reduction should be specified in terms of the capital letter height required on the finished sign. Provided that the panel dimensions on the artwork have been determined in relation to the x-height of the lettering as suggested in Chapter 4, then the finished panel will automatically be the correct size.*
5 *The completed artwork should be protected by a cover sheet, on which the name and address of the owner can be conveniently placed.*

Chapter six **Publications and stationery**

Publications and stationery should be coordinated with one another in a distinctive house style, and where possible they should also be visually linked in some way with the signing system. This link might simply be a similar approach to the layout of information, or it might be a stronger association brought about by the use of the signing type face for headings in publications or even for the text. It would be unwise, however, to restrict the choice of type faces to be used for publications too severely. In some situations it may be desirable to use a completely different type face to attract attention, or to link certain publications which form a distinct set and to differentiate them from other publications in the total range.

Publications

Production methods

Given that relatively small print runs are generally required for library publications, the most economical and convenient way of producing a result of acceptable quality will be to have the text set on an IBM Composer and the copies printed on a small offset-litho press. Photosetting or hot-metal setting would undoubtedly result in superior quality, but they are both considerably more expensive than IBM setting, and it is doubtful whether the difference would be appreciated by the majority of users.

The IBM Composer is a sophisticated golfball typewriter. Golfballs are available for a number of conventional type faces in a range of text sizes and weights. The output consists of proportionally spaced lettering, typed at the required line spacing and to the required measure, on high quality paper. Text in this form is known as 'repro'.

Any information (such as the title or main headings within the text) which needs to be in a type size substantially larger than that of the text will need to be produced separately. Dry-transfer lettering, photosetting or hot-metal setting may be used. Photosetting may be preferable to hot-metal setting for some purposes as it will generally give a wider choice of display faces. The headings and text will then need to be brought together by 'pasting-up' (see p143). The printer will photograph the paste-ups in order to produce litho plates for printing.

The printer will generally recommend suit-

131

| A2 | A3 |
| A4 | A5 |

International paper sizes (mm)

	A series	B series	C series
0	1189 x 841	1414 x 1000	1297 x 917
1	841 x 594	1000 x 707	917 x 648
2	594 x 420	707 x 500	648 x 458
3	420 x 297	500 x 353	458 x 324
4	297 x 210	353 x 250	324 x 229
5	210 x 148	250 x 176	229 x 162
6	148 x 105	176 x 125	162 x 114
7	105 x 74	125 x 88	114 x 81
8	74 x 52	88 x 62	81 x 57
9	52 x 37	62 x 44	
10	37 x 26	44 x 31	

1/3 A size

2/3 A size

able papers. If tinted papers are used, the tint should be very light or the contrast between the print and paper will be reduced and legibility may be impaired. Similarly, if inks other than black are used, they should be very dark in colour.

Page formats

In choosing page formats for publications, it is wise to base them on International Standard Paper Sizes. These sizes have the advantage of being readily available, and printers will have no difficulty in handling them. Indeed, some of the equipment used by small-offset printers will accept only International sizes.

There are three series of sizes. The A series is intended for publications and stationery and

Above: *The A series of International Paper Sizes, showing how each size has half the area of the next largest size.*
Right: *Acceptable divisions of A sizes.*
Left: *Dimensions of sizes in the A, B and C series.*

the B series for magazines and posters. The C series relates to envelopes, which are designed to take the A series of paper sizes. Each range of sizes is built up by halving the longest dimension of the largest size and using this as the shortest dimension of the next size down. The longest dimension of this size is then halved, and so on.

A4 and A5 are the most useful basic sizes for publications. This does not mean that these are the only possible page sizes however. A sizes can be divided into thirds, and the additional sizes thereby created can be very useful for certain kinds of publications. For example, an A4 sheet, folded into three to give three 1/3 A4 'pages', is ideal for many kinds of leaflet, while 2/3 A4 is useful for books and booklets.

Page grids

In order to achieve a professional result, it is important to define the boundaries of the information on each page by means of a grid. All text, tables and illustrations should fit into this grid exactly.

The simplest grids consist of a single column of information per page. Appropriate proportions for the information area in relation to the total page area will vary in relation to the nature of the publication. The proportions of the so-called 'Classical' grid are based almost entirely on aesthetic principles. Traditional ratios be-tween the sizes of the margins are 1 (inner margin), 1½ (head margin), 2 (foredge) and 2½ (foot margin), or 1½, 2, 3 and 4. The margins are relatively generous, and the information area may account for only 50 per cent of the total page area. Margins of this depth have not been shown to be essential for legibility, however, and they are expensive because so much of the page area is unused. 'Economical' grids with narrower margins, often of equal depth, are therefore popular for many kinds of publication. It must be remembered, however, that certain kinds of binding (such as ring binders and plastic slide binders) will require a relatively wide inner margin. Alternatives to the single-column grid include two- and three-column grids, which may be either symmetrical or asymmetrical, and the four-column grid.

There are several factors to be considered in choosing a grid, one of which is the nature and structure of the information. Single-column grids are suitable for text with tables and illustrations which will occupy the full column width. Two-column grids are useful for text with tables and illustrations which vary in size and which will either fit exactly into one column or across both columns. Three-column grids give considerable flexibility, as tables and illustrations can have a width of one, two or three columns. Still more flexibility can be obtained by superimposing a two- and a three-column grid. Four-column grids are particularly suitable for information which requires only a

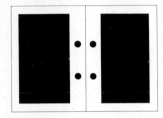

Above left: *The 'Classical' grid with traditional margins.*
Above: *The economical grid, with narrow margins.*
Left: *A grid with relatively wide inner margins to allow for binding.*
Below: *Symmetrical and asymmetrical grids.*

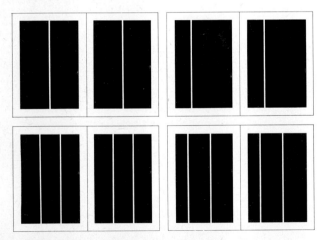

short line length. Bibliographies and indexes are examples of this kind of information.

Before a final choice is made, however, it is essential to consider the grid in relation to the proposed page size. Allowance should be made for reasonably generous margins, as this will give the page a much more open and inviting appearance. This done, the line length per column can be calculated. Whether or not the line length is acceptable will depend on the choice of type size. This is discussed on p 135.

Type face

If IBM setting is used, a seriffed face will give much more satisfactory results. This is because of the nature of the letter spacing system on the IBM Composer. Narrow letters such as 'i' and 'l' are relatively generously spaced, and this is especially noticeable with sans serif faces. Serifs help to fill in the spaces adjacent to narrow letters, thereby creating an apparently more even texture. The most popular IBM faces are Press Roman and Baskerville. If there are strong reasons for using a sans serif face, Univers is available.

Type size

Nine, 10 and 11 point are all suitable type sizes for text. On the IBM Composer, Press Roman is available in all three of these sizes, and Baskerville is available in 9 and 11 point. Ten point is generally regarded as an optimum size, but 9 point is acceptable where space is limited, and 11 point is advisable if the library is used by a significant number of older readers whose eyesight may be failing.

The final choice will depend to some extent on the type face. At any given size, Press Roman has a larger x-height than Baskerville. This means that 9 or 10 point Press Roman can often be used in situations where 9 point Baskerville would not be large enough, yet 11 point Baskerville would be too large. The choice of text size must also be considered in relation to any restrictions on line length imposed by the choice of grid.

The use of bold type in the text size (together with suitable spacing) will often be sufficient to emphasise subheadings in the text. The structure of the text will be clearer, however, if main headings are emphasised by the use of a larger type size. The difference in size should be immediately obvious to the reader, and suitable sizes will be within the range 18 to 36 point. Even larger sizes can be used with good effect where the lettering is serving a primarily decorative purpose, as on the cover of a leaflet for example.

Line length

The optimum line length for printed text is one which contains between 50 and 65 characters and spaces, or about nine to eleven words. Very

short lines will disrupt the normal pattern of eye movements in reading and will prevent efficient use of peripheral vision. Very long lines, on the other hand, will make it difficult for the eyes to accurately locate the beginning of each new line after the backsweep from the end of the previous line.

Ideally, therefore, the line length (or measure) should be such that it accommodates an optimum number of characters or words in the chosen type face and size. If this ideal is to be achieved, the page size, grid and type size must be chosen in relation to one another.

If the page size and grid have already been decided upon and they are such that the line length is relatively short, it may be necessary to opt for 9 point type in order to fit enough characters into each line. With a longer line, on the other hand, 9 point type might result in too many characters per line, and it would then be advisable to use a larger type size.

Alternatively, if a firm decision has already been made on the type size, it may be necessary to reconsider the choice of grid and/or the page size in order to achieve a satisfactory line length.

Line spacing

The terminology used by printers in specifying line spacing originally arose in relation to metal type. With founders' type, which is set by hand, an appropriate amount of space between lines is created by the type body, which extends beyond the upper and lower limits of the letter itself (see Chapter 2). When each line of type is butted up to the next, the type is said to be 'set solid'. If more space is required between lines, thin strips of lead are inserted. The thickness of these strips is measured in points, thus one might specify '9 point type, 1 point leaded'. With machine setting, the same effect is achieved by casting the type on a larger body. In this case, one would specify '9 on 10 point type'. Both of these ways of specifying line spacing are also used in relation to photoset type, even though there is no type body and no leading as such.

The use of leading or additional space between lines has the effect of increasing the maximum line length which will be acceptable for type of a given size. This is because the lines are more clearly differentiated from one another, thus making it easier for the eye to move unhesitatingly and accurately from the end of one line to the beginning of the next. Leading will therefore be particularly helpful to the reader in situations where the type size is relatively small in relation to the measure (or the measure is relatively large in relation to the type size). Leading will be less helpful with larger type sizes or narrower measures, but 1 or 2 points of leading will always have a positive rather than a negative effect on legibility with type sizes between 9 and 11 points.

The relation between word spacing and line spacing must also be considered. If the text is to be set solid, then word spacing must be kept to a minimum. If rather more generous word spacing is required, then 1 or 2 points of leading must be added.

Justification

Justification of the right-hand margin is not recommended. As suggested in Chapter 2, the resulting hyphenations and variations in letter and word spacing are aesthetically displeasing and may reduce legibility, particularly with relatively short measures. Furthermore, right-hand justification is inappropriate with the ranged-left layouts recommended here, and it will increase the setting time and hence the production costs.

The relation between type size, line length and leading.

A measure as short as 16 picas is acceptable with 9 point type, but a 24 pica measure will be too long unless one or preferably two points of leading are used. Where space permits, one point leading is also recommended for the shorter measure and for all intermediate line lengths. (1 pica = 12 points, ie 1/6 in or approximately 4 mm)

9 point Press Roman Medium Latin

	16 picas	24 picas
9 point set solid	Most books or articles in journals, when they have been fully identified, can be borrowed from other libraries if they are not in the College library stock. To use this service, fill in a blue form for a book or a pink form for a journal. Give the source of the reference, that is to say,	Most books or articles in journals, when they have been fully identified, can be borrowed from other libraries if they are not in the College library stock. To use this service, fill in a blue form for a book or a pink form for a journal. Give the source of the reference, that is to say,
9 on 10 point	Most books or articles in journals, when they have been fully identified, can be borrowed from other libraries if they are not in the College library stock. To use this service, fill in a blue form for a book or a pink form for a journal. Give the source of the reference, that is to say,	Most books or articles in journals, when they have been fully identified, can be borrowed from other libraries if they are not in the College library stock. To use this service, fill in a blue form for a book or a pink form for a journal. Give the source of the reference, that is to say,
9 on 11 point	Most books or articles in journals, when they have been fully identified, can be borrowed from other libraries if they are not in the College library stock. To use this service, fill in a blue form for a book or a pink form for a journal. Give the source of the reference, that is to say,	Most books or articles in journals, when they have been fully identified, can be borrowed from other libraries if they are not in the College library stock. To use this service, fill in a blue form for a book or a pink form for a journal. Give the source of the reference, that is to say,

10 point Press Roman Medium Latin

	16 picas	*24 picas*
10 point set solid	Most books or articles in journals, when they have been fully identified, can be borrowed from other libraries if they are not in the College library stock. To use this service, fill in a blue form for a book or a pink form for a journal. Give the source of the reference, that is to say,	Most books or articles in journals, when they have been fully identified, can be borrowed from other libraries if they are not in the College library stock. To use this service, fill in a blue form for a book or a pink form for a journal. Give the source of the reference, that is to say,
10 on 11 point	Most books or articles in journals, when they have been fully identified, can be borrowed from other libraries if they are not in the College library stock. To use this service, fill in a blue form for a book or a pink form for a journal. Give the source of the reference, that is to say,	Most books or articles in journals, when they have been fully identified, can be borrowed from other libraries if they are not in the College library stock. To use this service, fill in a blue form for a book or a pink form for a journal. Give the source of the reference, that is to say,
10 on 12 point	Most books or articles in journals, when they have been fully identified, can be borrowed from other libraries if they are not in the College library stock. To use this service, fill in a blue form for a book or a pink form for a journal. Give the source of the reference, that is to say,	Most books or articles in journals, when they have been fully identified, can be borrowed from other libraries if they are not in the College library stock. To use this service, fill in a blue form for a book or a pink form for a journal. Give the source of the reference, that is to say,

This page: *Both the 16 and the 24 pica measure are acceptable with 10 point type, though an intermediate measure would be preferable. The use of leading will greatly improve the legibility of text set to a 24 pica measure, and it is also recommended for shorter measures.*

Opposite page: *A 16 pica measure is too short for good legibility with 11 point type, whereas a 24 pica line length is ideal. The use of one point leading is recommended for the 24 pica measure, and it will enhance the appearance of text set to shorter line lengths.*

	16 picas	*24 picas*
11 point set solid	Most books or articles in journals, when they have been fully identified, can be borrowed from other libraries if they are not in the College library stock. To use this service, fill in a blue form for a book or a pink form for a journal. Give the source of the reference, that is to say,	Most books or articles in journals, when they have been fully identified, can be borrowed from other libraries if they are not in the College library stock. To use this service, fill in a blue form for a book or a pink form for a journal. Give the source of the reference, that is to say,
11 on 12 point	Most books or articles in journals, when they have been fully identified, can be borrowed from other libraries if they are not in the College library stock. To use this service, fill in a blue form for a book or a pink form for a journal. Give the source of the reference, that is to say,	Most books or articles in journals, when they have been fully identified, can be borrowed from other libraries if they are not in the College library stock. To use this service, fill in a blue form for a book or a pink form for a journal. Give the source of the reference, that is to say,
11 on 13 point	Most books or articles in journals, when they have been fully identified, can be borrowed from other libraries if they are not in the College library stock. To use this service, fill in a blue form for a book or a pink form for a journal. Give the source of the reference, that is to say,	Most books or articles in journals, when they have been fully identified, can be borrowed from other libraries if they are not in the College library stock. To use this service, fill in a blue form for a book or a pink form for a journal. Give the source of the reference, that is to say,

	16 picas	24 picas
9 point set solid	Most books or articles in journals, when they have been fully identified, can be borrowed from other libraries if they are not in the College library stock. To use this service, fill in a blue form for a book or a pink form for a journal. Give the source of the reference, that is to say,	Most books or articles in journals, when they have been fully identified, can be borrowed from other libraries if they are not in the College library stock. To use this service, fill in a blue form for a book or a pink form for a journal. Give the source of the reference, that is to say,
9 on 10 point	Most books or articles in journals, when they have been fully identified, can be borrowed from other libraries if they are not in the College library stock. To use this service, fill in a blue form for a book or a pink form for a journal. Give the source of the reference, that is to say,	Most books or articles in journals, when they have been fully identified, can be borrowed from other libraries if they are not in the College library stock. To use this service, fill in a blue form for a book or a pink form for a journal. Give the source of the reference, that is to say,
9 on 11 point	Most books or articles in journals, when they have been fully identified, can be borrowed from other libraries if they are not in the College library stock. To use this service, fill in a blue form for a book or a pink form for a journal. Give the source of the reference, that is to say,	Most books or articles in journals, when they have been fully identified, can be borrowed from other libraries if they are not in the College library stock. To use this service, fill in a blue form for a book or a pink form for a journal. Give the source of the reference, that is to say,

This page: *A 16 pica measure is suitable for 9 point Baskerville, but a 24 pica measure will be uncomfortably long unless at least one point of leading is used. Leading is also desirable with shorter measures, but as a general rule Baskerville will need less leading than Press Roman because of its smaller x-height. It is therefore particularly suitable for use where limitations on space demand that the text should be set solid or only one point leaded.*

Opposite page: *As with Press Roman type, a 16 pica measure is too short for optimum legibility with 11 point Baskerville. A line length approaching 24 picas is much more suitable. The text can be set solid if necessary, but the use of leading is to be preferred.*

	16 picas	24 picas
11 point set solid	Most books or articles in journals, when they have been fully identified, can be borrowed from other libraries if they are not in the College library stock. To use this service, fill in a blue form for a book or a pink form for a journal. Give the source of the reference, that is to say,	Most books or articles in journals, when they have been fully identified, can be borrowed from other libraries if they are not in the College library stock. To use this service, fill in a blue form for a book or a pink form for a journal. Give the source of the reference, that is to say,
11 on 12 point	Most books or articles in journals, when they have been fully identified, can be borrowed from other libraries if they are not in the College library stock. To use this service, fill in a blue form for a book or a pink form for a journal. Give the source of the reference, that is to say,	Most books or articles in journals, when they have been fully identified, can be borrowed from other libraries if they are not in the College library stock. To use this service, fill in a blue form for a book or a pink form for a journal. Give the source of the reference, that is to say,
11 on 13 point	Most books or articles in journals, when they have been fully identified, can be borrowed from other libraries if they are not in the College library stock. To use this service, fill in a blue form for a book or a pink form for a journal. Give the source of the reference, that is to say,	Most books or articles in journals, when they have been fully identified, can be borrowed from other libraries if they are not in the College library stock. To use this service, fill in a blue form for a book or a pink form for a journal. Give the source of the reference, that is to say,

The layout of text, tabular matter and illustrations must conform with the chosen grid at all times. The treatment of headings, captions, footnotes etc will also be influenced by the choice of grid.

With an asymmetrical double-column grid, for example, it is often convenient to use the narrower column for headings, or perhaps for footnotes or captions to illustrations. Where necessary, tables and illustrations can extend across both columns, but the main text will always occupy the second column only.

With a symmetrical grid, it will be necessary to integrate the headings with the text. Where tables or illustrations run across both columns, the double-column layout is still retained for the text.

Alternative treatments of the same information using symmetrical and asymmetrical two-column grids. Notice that although the table extends across both columns of the symmetrical grid, the spacing of the columns within the table has not been increased.

Official publications The collection of British Government publications, together with those of various International Organisations, is kept in the Official Publications Room on Floor 1. Basically they are divided into a periodical and a monograph sequence and within each of these the arrangement is by the organisation issuing the publication. A booklet giving more details of this collection is available from the enquiry desk.

Reference books and bibliographies Located on Floor 1, this section contains the most important encyclopedias, dictionaries, biographical dictionaries, directories, glossaries and indexes in every field covered by the Library, together with general and special bibliographies, major library catalogues and lists of periodicals.

Special Collections These are kept in the room to the rear of the enquiry desk. They include the Ketton-Cremer collection on Norfolk history, a collection on military history given by the de Saumarez family of Suffolk, an illustrated books collection, and the Abbot collection of editions of English literature.

Theses The Library collection of UEA PhD and MPhil theses is housed in the special collections room. Application should be made to the enquiry desk. The theses can be consulted in the Library only.

Videotapes The Library possesses a Sony Videorecorder machine linked to a transistor TV for the playing of videotapes. The machine and the Library's collection of tapes, are housed in the audio-visual area.

Microforms The Library possesses collections of material in microform and various machines for reading them. They are located in the audio-visual area.

Pamphlets These are shelved in boxes separate from, but on the same floor as, the books on the same subject. The charts at the entrance to each floor show the exact locations. Many pamphlets are recorded in a catalogue following the subject catalogue.

Oversize books These are shelved in special sequences on the same floor as other books on the same subject.

Music scores These are shelved with the literature of music on Floor 3, but are recorded in a separate catalogue next to the pamphlets catalogue.

Catalogues Periodicals are not recorded in the card catalogue, but in a series of visible indexes. There is a general index on Floor 1, and sectional indexes on the floors to which they relate, which list, in alphabetical order, the title of each journal and the number and date of the earliest volume held, thus: JOURNAL OF MOLECULAR BIOLOGY, 1 1959. Gaps in the holdings are indicated either as 30 - 39, 1950 - 55, 39, 1958 ..., or by the word 'Incompl.' A record of incomplete sets is kept in the periodicals office.

Periodicals The arrangement and location of periodicals are indicated in the following chart.

Subject	Class Bound	Unbound	Floor
Bibliography	Z	Z	1
Biology	Q	QH	01
Chemistry	Q	QD	01
Computer science	Q	QX	01
Environmental sciences	Q	QU	01
Fine arts	N	N	3
General	A	A	2
General science	Q	Q	01
History Economic history	D	D	2
Literature	P	P	3
Mathematics Physics	Q	QC	1
Music	M	M	3
Philosophy/Religion	B	B	2
Social sciences	G	G	2

Current issues Current issues and unbound parts of current volumes are kept apart from, but on the same floor as, the bound sets. They are sub-divided by subject (as shown above), and the unbound parts are shelved beneath the display of the current issues.

Newspapers Newspapers and weeklies will be found in the concourse. Files of back numbers are available on request.

Artwork for publications

The preparation of artwork is described here for a page consisting of a piece of text in repro form and a main heading in dry-transfer lettering.

1 Prepare an accurate layout as described in Chapter 5. Guidelines should be drawn for the dry-transfer lettering and the text, and the wording of the heading should be traced in full.

2 Obtain a piece of mounting board which is large enough to allow generous margins around the image area, and tape it squarely to the drawing board. Use the layout sheet to help in positioning the artwork in the centre of the mounting board, and draw guidelines for the dry-transfer lettering and the repro in light blue pencil. The horizontal guidelines for the repro should indicate the position of the base of the x-height of the first line. The vertical guidelines should mark the left and right-hand boundaries of the type area. Add trim marks in ink.

3 Lay the dry-transfer lettering as described in Chapter 5.

4 Trim the edges of the repro if necessary, leaving generous margins where possible. Place the edge of a ruler along the base of the x-height of the first line of type and mark this position on the left and right edges of the repro using a scalpel. (The marks made by a scalpel will be more precise than those from a pencil.) Next, position the ruler along the left hand edge of the text and make alignment marks on the top and bottom edges of the repro.

5 Cover the area of the artwork to receive the repro, and the back of the repro itself, with a *thin* film of Cow Gum. (Flexible plastic spreaders made for this specific purpose are readily available.) Leave the gum to dry for about ten minutes.

6 Place a sheet of dry-transfer backing paper over the gummed area of the artwork, leaving only the top half inch or so exposed. This will prevent the two surfaces from adhering prematurely. Carefully align the repro using the alignment marks and the guidelines. It is essential that the repro should be square with the artwork, as any error will be immediately obvious in print. When the alignment is satisfactory, lightly tack the top half inch of the repro onto the mounting board with the fingers. This done, gently pull away the backing sheet from between the repro and the artwork and place it over the repro. Burnish the whole area firmly with the hand.

7 Remove any excess Cow gum from around the edges of the repro by picking it up with a small ball of dry gum. (The dried residue left on the spreader, rolled into a ball, will serve the purpose.) The gum rubber should be used gently, taking great care not to lift the edges or corners of the repro. (If the margins on the repro are too narrow, there will be a risk of damaging the lettering at this stage.)

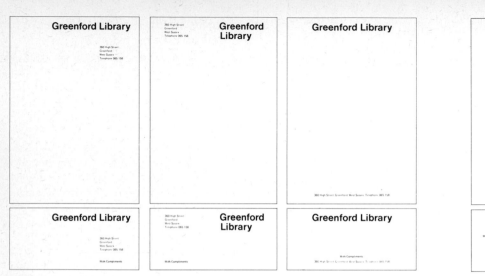

Examples of layouts for stationery carrying a logotype

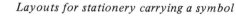

Layouts for stationery carrying a symbol

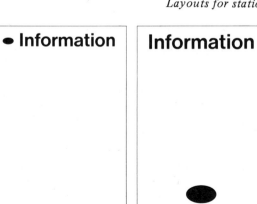

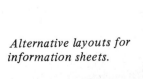

Alternative layouts for information sheets.

Sometimes it may be necessary to make corrections to the repro if it contains typing errors. Substantial corrections will often mean that the repro must be pasted-up in several pieces. Great care must be taken to ensure that the horizontal alignment of such pieces is correct, and that the line spacing and paragraph spacing remain consistent. Small corrections, however, are often easier to make after the repro has been pasted up. The offending word(s) or line(s) are carefully cut out with a scalpel and lifted away from the mounting board. The corrections are Cow-gummed, cut to size after the gum has dried, and carefully inserted into the gaps. Under no circumstances should corrections be pasted on top of the repro, as they can easily be accidentally dislodged.

Instructions to the printer should be written clearly and concisely on the edge of the mounting board outside the image area. In this way they cannot become separated from the artwork. The enlargement or reduction required should be stated in terms of the length of the longest dimension when printed. If the artwork is the correct size, this is usually indicated by specifying 's/s'. The ink colour and the size, colour and type of paper required should be given, and the printing method to be used should be confirmed. Finally, as much information as is necessary to uniquely identify the piece of artwork should be supplied. The name and telephone number of a person who may be contacted if any queries should arise will also be useful.

145

It is essential to keep the artwork clean. The high-contrast photographic materials used in this kind of work will pick up any dark smudges or other marks. A protective cover sheet should therefore be added.

Stationery

The type face used for library stationery should harmonise with that used for publications. Depending on the type face required, the wording can either be IBM typeset or photoset. In either case, offset lithography will be the most suitable reproduction method. Alternatively, hot-metal setting can be used, together with letterpress printing. This will give a crisper image, but may prove to be rather more expensive. This will almost certainly be the case if a logotype or symbol is used.

Useful page sizes for stationery are A4 and A5 for notepaper, 1/3A4 for compliments slips and A8 for visiting cards. A4 is also a very useful size for information sheets of various kinds.

The wording can either be ranged left or centred, but the ranged-left layout gives more freedom in the positioning of both the wording and the logotype or symbol on the page. Several of the many possible arrangements for stationery and information sheets are shown here.

Chapter seven **Project management**

Project planning

Before starting work on a signing project, and particularly if it is a large one, it is important to draw up a schedule showing what needs to be done, when, and by whom. Careful planning of this kind will help in making estimates of the amount of staff time required and the overall period which will be necessary for completion of the project. It is difficult to make generalisations about the programme of work because libraries differ so greatly in their signing requirements and in their resources, but the major stages in a signing project might be summarised as follows.

1 Background research
1.1 Collect and analyse background information about the library and its users
2 Preliminary planning
2.1 Determine the number of different kinds or groups of sign required
2.2 Determine the provisional location and content of all signs required; test these as necessary using mock-ups
2.3 Develop a provisional design scheme for each group of signs (typography, panel sizes, layout, symbols and colour)

2.4 Specify provisional placement for each group of signs
2.5 Investigate methods and materials for professional and/or in-house manufacture and fixing
3 Final planning
3.1 Finalise the location and content of each sign
3.2 Finalise the design of each group of signs and each individual sign
3.3 Finalise the placement of each group of signs and each individual sign
3.4 Finalise the choice of methods and materials for sign manufacture and fixing
4 Implementation
4.1 Prepare specifications for signs to be professionally manufactured, and seek cost estimates
4.2 Order equipment and materials for signs to be manufactured in-house
4.3 Prepare artwork (if necessary) for signs to be professionally manufactured and submit to the selected manufacturer
4.4 Carry out the manufacture of signs to be produced in-house
4.5 Install all signs
5 Evaluation

146

5.1 Evaluate the completed system in terms of the extent to which it solves the problems it was intended to solve

5.2 Carry out any minor modifications suggested by the results of the evaluation

6 Documentation

6.1 Prepare the sign manual

In a small signing project, some of these stages might well be omitted or combined with one another; in a large project, additional stages may be necessary.

The preparation of a sign manual

It is inevitable that at some stage additional or replacement signs will be required as a result of changes in the library and hence in the information to be given, or as a result of damage or wear and tear. Temporary signs in particular will be needed relatively frequently.

It is essential that any new signs, whether temporary or permanent, should be designed and manufactured in exactly the same way as the originals or the unity of the system will be lost. It will therefore be necessary to prepare a sign manual which gives full details of the design and manufacture of signs of each kind. Only in this way can the system be kept intact in future years when those responsible for its design and

implementation are perhaps no longer available to consult.

The manual should provide the following information.

1 A definition for each sign group

2 Any rules applicable to the choice of wording

3 Specifications for type face, type weight(s), letter form (capitals versus lower case), arrows, symbols, type sizes, panel sizes, panel layout, colour of background and lettering.

4 The principles of sign placement

5 Details of the materials and methods of manufacture used, together with the names and addresses of suppliers and manufacturers

6 Details of the methods of fixing used

Much of this information will need to be given in the form of illustrations with supporting text. The type face and weights, arrows and symbols should be illustrated. The relation between type size and panel size should be demonstrated by means of scale drawings labelled with appropriate measurements, and representative examples of panel layouts should be shown. The principles of sign placement should be illustrated, and diagrams of sign construction and fixings should be included if necessary.

In many cases it will be preferable to deal

with each group of signs separately, so that when the need for a new sign arises, all the information on the design and manufacture of that particular type of sign is together in one place.

Evaluating the completed system

When the system has been installed, it may be felt necessary to evaluate its effectiveness in some way. This will be a particularly worthwhile exercise where the system is just the first stage of a larger scheme.

The success of the system can only be measured in terms of the extent to which it fulfils its intended purpose, whether this was to change the image of the library, to reduce the number of simple enquiries dealt with by staff, to solve a particular direction-finding problem, or to improve the appearance of all or part of the library. Interviews and/or questionnaires might be used to gauge the overall reactions of users and staff and to elicit more specific comments on the information content and the design of the system. The content and the functional aspects of the design might be further investigated by repeating any other studies carried out before the project began, for example, observations of user behaviour, experiments on direction-finding and the use of instructions, and monitoring of enquiries.

Results before and after the installation of the new system can then be compared.

Provided that sufficient background research was carried out initially and that preliminary ideas on sign location, content, design and placement were tested out where necessary, the results of the evaluation should not hold any major surprises. They will, however, indicate the extent to which the objectives of the system have been met, and they may reveal any minor flaws which need correction and which should be avoided if the system is subsequently to be extended.

Employing a professional designer

If the intention is to employ a professional graphic designer, then the earlier he or she is involved in the project the better. If the designer is not involved from the beginning, then inevitably certain decisions will have been made which will limit his freedom, and he will not be able to use his analytical and creative skills to the full. Certainly it is possible to find designers who will be content to design and implement a system for which the content and even some of the design variables have already been finally decided upon, but this is not making the best use of the skills which the designer has to offer. Although it is the librarian's responsibility to accurately identify the problems which the new system is intended to solve, a good designer will want to begin by understanding these problems and by studying the proposed information content of the system very carefully. If the content is not complete and logically presented, then the designer cannot be expected to be able to represent it in a visually coherent fashion. In many cases, careful consideration of the problems of visually presenting a piece of information will reveal flaws in the logic behind it or will suggest that the information should be restructured so that it can be presented more clearly and hence be more easily understood. It is important, therefore, that the exact content of the system should not be finally decided upon until the design problems have been considered. Hence the need to involve the designer at an early stage.

Before beginning the search for a suitable designer, it is important that the librarian should have a clear idea of the purpose of the new system in terms of the problems it is intended to solve and any additional advantages which are hoped for. He or she should also be clear as to the role he wishes the designer to play. Will the designer be working with the library staff in finding a solution which will best meet the library's needs, or will he merely be implementing a solution which has already been partially determined? An outline of the problem and of the proposed roles of the library staff and the designer should be drawn up on paper to serve as a preliminary brief. The search for the designer can then begin.

One of the most common methods of finding a designer is by word of mouth. A recommendation from a colleague who has used a particular designer successfully on a similar project is ideal. Failing this, sign manufacturers are often able to recommend designers from whom they have received work of a similar kind. Alternatively, both the Design Council and the Society of Industrial Artists and Designers offer a designer selection service. In using such services it is important to state that the project is concerned with library signing (in the hope that a designer with experience of a similar project will be available), and to explain the scope of the project and the level at which the designer will be expected to involve himself. The result of such an enquiry will probably be a list of four or five likely design practices or individual designers.

The next step will be to make contact with the designers suggested by these various sources and to discuss the project with them briefly over the telephone. This may eliminate some of them, perhaps because the practice no longer has a designer with appropriate experience, or because they cannot undertake to carry out the work immediately, or because their fees would exceed by far the sum available.

The most likely two or three designers might then be invited to visit the library to see the problem at first hand and to discuss it in more detail. Any who do not withdraw or who are not rejected at this stage should then be asked to submit a proposal for the work, based on the preliminary brief drawn up by the librarian, plus any agreed amendments. The proposal should include a statement of the designer's understanding of the problem, an outline of the approach to be taken in solving it, a provisional programme of work, and an indication of the likely fees at each stage.

When the final selection has been made on the basis of the proposals submitted, a final brief should be agreed with the designer. This brief and the designer's proposal will form the basis of the contract between the two parties, and they should be referred to in the letter of appointment. In larger projects it may be desirable for the project to proceed in a series of stages, each stage to be satisfactorily completed before agreement is given for the next stage to commence. This kind of provision might also be written into the letter of appointment.

Once work has begun on the project, it is the librarian's responsibility to give the designer all the help he can in terms of providing background information. Unless the designer has been employed merely as a technician, the librarian must also be prepared for any preconceptions he may have about the content of the system to be questioned. As an outsider, the designer will often be aware of potential sources of confusion and misunderstanding which library staff who are familiar with the building and its contents may not be aware of. If he did not question any preconceptions which he felt to be a potential threat to the success of the system, he would not be behaving in a professional manner.

Finally, it must be emphasised that the first concern of a good designer will be to produce a system within the agreed budget which is functional, aesthetically pleasing and in keeping with the character of the library. It will not be his aim to make his own personal mark on the library at the expense of all other considerations.

Appendix   Manufacturers and suppliers

Materials and equipment for in-house sign production

Allied Manufacturing Company (London) Limited

Sarena House, Grove Park,
Colindale, London NW9
Tel (01) 205 8844
Telex 23719

Ashwood (Graphics) Limited

153 Reading Road, Henley on
Thames, Oxfordshire
Tel (049 12) 78187

Autotype International Limited

Grove Road, Wantage,
Oxfordshire
Tel Wantage (023 57) 66251

Autotype USA

1380 Brummel Avenue, Elk
Grove Village, Illinois 60007,
USA
Tel 0101 (312) 5931955

Balmforth Engineering Limited

Library Systems Division,
Finway, Dallows Road, Luton,
Bedfordshire LUI ITE
Tel Luton (0582) 31171

Chartpak Europe

Station Road, Didcot,
Oxfordshire OXII 7NB
Tel Didcot (0235) 812607

Gaylord Brothers Incorporated

Box 4901, Syracuse, NY 13221,
USA
Tel 0101 (315) 4575070

Graphic Systems International

1/7 Cornwallis Road, Alleney
Road Industrial Estate, Lincoln
LN3 4RD
Tel Lincoln (0522) 36131/2
Telex 56439

Don Gresswell Limited

Bridge House, Grange Park,
London N21 1RB
Tel (01) 360 6622/4

GW Film Sales

Britannia Works, Woolwich
Industrial Estate, 8 Kellner Road,
London SE28 OAX
Tel (01) 855 9051   Telex 898051

Hartley Reece and Company

Building One, GEC Estate, East
Lane, Wembley, Middlesex
HA9 7PY
Tel (01) 908 2577

IBM United Kingdom Limited

101 Wigmore Street, London
W1H OAB
Tel (01) 935 6600

Letraset UK Limited

195-203 Waterloo Road, London
SE1
Tel (01) 928 7551

Libraco Limited

Lombard Wall, London SE7
Tel (01) 858 3308

Librex Educational Company

Colwick Low Road, Nottingham
NG2 4BG
Tel Nottingham (0602) 54664/
50032

Mecanorma Limited

10 School Road, London NW10
Tel (0l) 961 6565   Telex 22623

Movitex Signs Limited

107 High Street, Edgware,
Middlesex HA8 7HJ
Tel (01) 952 7681

Murographics Limited

Oldmixon Industrial Estate,
Weston-super-Mare, Avon
BS24 9AX
Tel Weston-super-Mare (0934)
32558   Telex 444563

**Olympia Business Machines
Company Limited**

203/205 Old Marylebone Road,
London NWl 5QS
Tel (01) 262 6788

152

Pelltech Limited

6 Church Green, Witney,
Oxfordshire
Tel Witney (0993) 72014

Philip and Tacey Limited

North Way, Andover,
Hampshire
Tel Andover (0264) 61171

**Pintype and Moulded Letter
Company**

51 Lisson Grove, London
NWl 6UJ
Tel (01) 723 3231

Sasco Limited

27 Hastings Road, Bromley,
Kent BR2 8NA
Tel (01) 462 2241

**Spur Systems International
Limited**

Spur House, Otterspool Way,
Watford, Hertfordshire WD2 8HT
Tel Watford (0923) 26071

Staedtler (UK) Limited

Pontyclun, Mid Glamorgan
CF7 8YJ
Tel Llantrisant (0443) 222421
Telex 497025

Techniform Display Limited

Crown Buildings, Crown Street,
London SE5
Tel (01) 703 0481

VariTyper Corporation

11 Mount Pleasant Avenue, East
Hanover, New Jersey 07936, USA
Tel 0101 (201) 8878000

A West and Partners Limited

684 Mitcham Road, Croydon
CR9 3AB
Tel (01) 684 6171   Telex 947938

Wondersigns Limited

Stockingswater Lane, Brimsdown,
Enfield, Middlesex
Tel (01) 804 2674

WW Instant Signs Limited

Harrington Road, South Norwood,
London SE25 4LX
Tel (01) 656 4511
Telex 8813368

Off-the-shelf systems

Bush Signs Limited

Beaconsfield Road, Brighton,
Sussex BN1 4QX
Tel Brighton (0273) 680197
Telex 877153

Esselte Dymo Limited

Spur Road, North Feltham
Trading Estate, Feltham,
Middlesex TW14 OSL
Tel (01) 890 1388
Telex 8814416

Don Gresswell Limited

Bridge House, Grange Park,
London N21 1RB
Tel (01) 360 6622/4

Metalcraft

Maze Street, Barton Hill, Bristol
Tel Bristol (0272) 552302

Spandex UK Limited

21 Portland Square, Bristol
BS2 8SJ
Tel Bristol (0272) 425942
Telex 44220

Syncronol Industries Limited

Blackbushe Trading Estate, off
Vigo Lane, Yateley, Camberley,
Surrey
Tel (0252) 872661/2/3
Telex 858428

WW Instant Signs Limited

Harrington Road, South Norwood,
London SE25 4LX
Tel (01) 656 4511
Telex 8813368

Professional sign manufacturers

Alan and Kenneth Breese

387 King Street, Hammersmith,
London W6 9NJ
Tel (01) 748 8896
*Lettering craftsmen specialising in
signwriting, engraving, inscribing
etc*

Bush Signs Limited

61 Beaconsfield Road, Brighton,
Sussex BN1 4QX
Tel Brighton (0273) 680197
Telex 877153
*Screen printing, sub-surface print-
ing, signwriting, etching, engraving,
three-dimensional lettering etc*

Falconcraft Limited

Hainault Road, Romford, Essex
RM5 3AH
Tel Romford (70) 24621/9
Telex 897108
*Screen printing, sub-surface print-
ing, engraving, etching, inscribing,
enamelling etc*

Graphex Industrial Art Limited

51 Lisson Grove, London NW1
Tel (01) 723 3231
*Screen printing, sub-surface print-
ing, engraving, inscribing, three-
dimensional lettering etc*

Lettercast Limited

Great Western Lane, Barton Hill,
Bristol BS5 9TH
Tel Bristol (0272) 553234
*Specialists in injection-moulded
plastic lettering*

Pearce Signs Limited

Insignia House, London SE14
Tel (01) 692 6611

Screen printing, sub-surface printing, signwriting, engraving, inscribing, three-dimensional lettering etc

Rivermeade (Importers) Limited

Oxford Road, Denham, Uxbridge
UB9 4NB
Tel Denham (0895) 834493
Telex 28148

Screen printing, signwriting, etching, engraving, inscribing, enamelling, three-dimensional lettering etc

Syncronol Industries Limited

Blackbushe Trading Estate, off
Vigo Lane, Yately, Camberley,
Surrey GU17 7ET
Tel Yateley (0252) 872661
Telex 858428

Specialists in screen printing and etching

Ward and Company (Letters) Limited

154

Maze Street, Barton Hill Trading
Estate, Barton Hill, Bristol
BS5 9TE
Tel Bristol (0272) 553774/553385

Screen printing, signwriting, engraving, photo-anodising, three-dimensional lettering etc

Wood and Wood International Signs Limited

Harrington Road, London
SE25 4LX
Tel (01) 656 4511
Telex 8813368

Screen printing, etching, engraving, enamelling, anodising, decal and three-dimensional lettering etc

Graphic arts suppliers

Colyer and Southey (Sales) Limited

24-28 Hatton Wall, London
EC1N 8JH
Tel (01) 242 0091

Hunter Penrose

7 Spa Road, London SE16 3QS
Tel (01) 237 6636   Telex 884654

London Graphics Centre

107 Long Acre, London WC2
Tel (01) 240 0235

WH Smith and Son Limited (Head Office)

10 New Fetter Lane, London EC4
Tel (01) 353 0277

Further reading

Corporate identity

Blake JE
A management guide to corporate identity
London: Council of Industrial Design 1971

Pilditch J
Communication by design: a study of corporate identity
Maidenhead: McGraw Hill 1970

Sign design and manufacture

Crosby/Fletcher/Forbes
A sign systems manual
London: Studio Vista Limited 1970

Dreyfuss H
Symbol sourcebook: an authoritative guide to international graphic symbols
New York: McGraw Hill 1972

Follis J and Hammar D
Architectural signing and graphics
London: The Architectural Press Limited 1979

Signs in libraries

Pollet D and Haskell P
Sign systems for libraries
London: RR Bowker Company 1979

Spencer H and Reynolds L
Directional signing and labelling in libraries and museums: a review of current theory and practice
London: Readability of Print Research Unit, Royal College of Art 1977

Design of publications

Dowding G
Finer points in the spacing and arrangement of type
London: Ernest Benn 1966

McLean R
Magazine design
Oxford: Oxford University Press 1969

Spencer H
The visible word
London: Lund Humphries 1969

Employing a graphic designer

Topalian A
Don't just hire the nice guy
Design 1977 November 50-51

Topalian A
Not paid to be nice guys
Design 1977 December 44-45

Index